I dedicate what you're about to read to my parents.

Without them, I never would have survived any of it.

<u>Special Thanks To:</u>

L.M.W
Patrick Norris
Katie Posch

In Memory of

Johnny "Butch" Rumoro III

Fly high to heaven brother. I am sure you're check-raising the poker Gods right now. See you when I'm dealt my final hand.

GAMBLING with DEMONS

&

DRINKING with the DEVIL

"Everything in life is worth living for."

65 Miles Outside of Vegas-

I-15 to Los Angeles had never been more vacant in its lifetime. It was its own ghost town as another mile passed me by. Granted, I had only drove that route from Vegas to L.A. twice, but to not see a single car for an entire hour didn't seem realistic to me. It was like the rest of the world just knew how drunk and exhausted I was, that they should stay off the highway for the night. All of us have at one point or another, gotten into a car and just put it into drive without a destination. You just cruise until you feel it necessary to turn around and go back to wherever it is that you came from. Only I never found a reason to turn around this time. My glass of gin had gone from the cup holder to between my legs for some reason. The rest of the bottle sat quietly on the seat next to me. The passenger window was cracked for some air and I hadn't turned the radio back on since I left Vegas about an hour before.

I couldn't understand what I had just been through and how it was all gone. Not just the money, but my pursuit for life as a whole. I had $180 left in my pocket, I owed over $160,000 to random people, yet I still loved the game more than life itself. None of it hit me yet. There wasn't going to be any more private jets or presidential suites. I didn't have the energy to borrow more money either. The hole I had buried myself in was going to take me years to get back on my feet. I was entirely terrified of what my future had in store for me. Gambling was all I knew, everyone knew that. I was possessed by it, almost as bad as the drinking. I couldn't really figure out which was worse at this point to be honest. The more I thought about it, though, I guess they're scaled differently. Both possessions were obviously way out of control. I had lost $1.7 million in the last couple of months and I barely remember any of it.

I finally decided to pull off to the side of the road and drive about a hundred feet into the desert. There wasn't a darker patch of land anywhere else on this planet than what lied out in front of me. I put the car in park and climbed out onto the gravel desert surface. It was amazing how I had just drove for about an hour, but I could still see Vegas' lights off in the distance combining with the sky above. It was quiet out here, but the thoughts that were running through my mind were louder than a scene of fireworks. I was numb about whatever it was that I was feeling. I think it was going to take me a while to realize how much I had just destroyed my life. The habits I had become used to had turned themselves into my own death sentence all on their own. I had an awfully high tolerance for not giving a fuck about anything as of lately. Then when you mix in the alcohol intake like usual and the amount of money I had lost in the last year, my desire and love for this town had vanished.

With the bottle in one hand, I climbed up to the top of the car and spread out and got comfortable. Well, as comfortable as I could get given the circumstances. All that was missing was some snow and I could make snow angels like I used to love doing when I was a kid. So many little things like that had made me such a happy kid once upon a time, but were now buried somewhere in my past. I missed all the little things in life that used to make me happy, that used to make me want to keep on living. But this overrated town had just become a graveyard to me. Filled with ghosts from my poker past that will go on to haunt me forever. Not necessarily people, but the episodes that kept playing in my head of the moments as it all went downhill. A string of awful bets and bad decisions became a never ending snowball effect that led me to where I am right now.

I was fucked, yet I couldn't convince myself just yet that I needed to call it quits already and admit that my time here was up. I had too much pride in myself because of the accomplishments and recognition I had received since I began this risky journey four years prior. I hit rock bottom and it still wasn't enough for me.

But, the alcohol never tasted this good. I felt like it was the only thing I had left. The little bit of cash I had remaining in my pocket wasn't even real to me anymore. Money had just become some sort of fuel to assist me in surviving. It was one of those ingredients that just kept me going. Now that it was gone, this bottle that sat next to me seemed like the only piece of life I had left.

So, I just lied there. My thoughts were awful and the tears began to fall and they didn't stop for what felt like hours. I began to stare off into space at the billions of stars that hang above me and somehow someway, I remembered everything from the beginning of this unforgettable journey. But it never used to always be like this, life wasn't always this terrifying. There were days where I just played poker. Where I was surrounded by good people and my friends were curious about my new life out here. There were days in the beginning when I was sober and healthy. The days were perfect and filled with success. There were days where I couldn't wait to wake up to do it all over again. When I still had passion and love for every hand I was dealt.

I finished the rest of my drink and started to drink the rest from the bottle instead. I lied back down with the bottle in my hand and began to stare off into the sky. My conscious took control over my body as my entire gambling career played out in front of me from day one. I had no choice but to sit back and watch one last time.

"It's better to look back on life and say: I can't believe that I did that. Than to look back and say 'what if' for the rest of your life."

Introduction-

It's nearing the end of summer here in Chicago of 2013. I think I have finally discovered the necessary compulsion to write this book. It seems like this is finally the appropriate time to put this memoir to a finale. I sit in my room with a glass of wine and a full stomach. I have recently become obsessed with cooking and had a desire to cook up some kabobs this evening. Mixed in with some onions and peppers of course, I think that is the only way to do it. In the end, it made for a delicious meal and preparation for the beginning of what seems to be an anticipated novel by many.

Now, I have to be honest here. I have attempted to write this book about twenty times, possibly more. Through notebook paper, on long flights, at the poker table, on my previous phones, but I never seemed to be able to get anywhere with any of it. Along the way I would have to stop because I would get emotional, lose motivation, drop back into unpleasant thoughts towards the end of my career or just simply think it's not worth it. So in the course of the last six years, this attempt has found failure many of times. But, I think it's a good thing.

For the stories you are about to read, at least from my attempts before, I didn't have any closure with the life I once lived. I didn't have any rebirth until now. I didn't find myself dancing in the kitchen to music or appreciating sunsets. I didn't appreciate any of the little things in life. I was still caught up on what might have been and how bad I fucked up. But, is that a good thing or a bad thing? I guess only your judgment will ever be able to determine such a decision.

I am not too certain how many times I am going to reread the things I write. Then go back and make corrections and change my mind on a thousand different scenarios. I have developed zero outlines for this book and plan on just typing out my thoughts as the stories, feelings and emotions eventually counteract with my current memories. I've wrote out about 24 titles for chapters that can be made into their own little sections, but that number is subject to change both ways. But man, I can't wait until this is all over and I can go back and read all of it. I am just as excited as you are to be honest. I am sure I will end up with carpel tunnel when this is all said and done. But, definitely well worth it in the end to get everything out on paper and siphoned from my heart, mind and past and into your hands for your viewing. I forewarn you! I have a million stories. And with one story, there may be a handful of stories inside of them. The chapters enclosed are just the ones that I felt made the cut.

There hadn't been a day since I left college that poker and gambling hadn't been a part of my life. Not so much anymore to be honest, and I truly mean that. I went a solid six years where there wasn't a day that went by that I didn't gamble somehow. It became a part of my life. From the pits, to all forms of poker, to props and sports betting, they were all an ingredient to an exquisite experience. Like how normal humans eat food and drink water to survive, I needed and did add gambling to that mix. It became a necessity and obligation to make myself feel alive. Obviously with maturing and experiences of my gambling career, things became more intense.

I'm going to swear and I'm going to be as graphic as I can in this story. This is definitely the last attempt I am ever going to make to finally complete this. That's a promise. So if no one ever reads this, I guess I gave up. But, if you're nestled somewhere on a couch and the book is crouched between your arms and you're about to read all of this, I guess I stuck to my promise and finally finished this fucking thing. I promise you, if that's the case, it's my most warm hearted accomplishment I have ever had the pleasure of in this life.

Now I have to admit, I will be drinking wine throughout this entire development. I became accustomed to it in a very random way. I had a huge crush on this girl from high school and she loved sushi. For whatever reason I heard that the only drink you can have with sushi, is wine. Given that rumor, I have come to know that statement is completely false and that Asia has some of the most delicious beer and other liquors to choose from. So, I had to learn to love both wine and sushi for her. She eventually didn't fall for me as expected. But, now I love wine and sushi! I feel like drinking will give me a better way to be more descriptive, honest and sincere if I am sipping back on some of grandpa's old cough medicine. If anything, it'll help me explore my old mind some more too. ALL names will be switched to fictional ones in these coming chapters for obvious reasons. I am sure if you are reading this and you were a part of my past to such a personal capacity, you will be able to figure out who you are. So, congratulations on that accomplishment. I capitalize "all" because I wanted to make that point clear as day right now. Zero names in this story will be accurate. The stories on the other hand, will be.

I understand that all of the household poker players these days, Negreanu, Ivey, Brunson and all the rest of them, they all have their own books out. Not even really about their life stories either, unless those have fell in the cracks from me. But about how to play the game and ways to better yourself in the different variations of poker we have available. The one thing that the public and even the poker world simply can't comply with, is that through those successful individuals, there's thousands upon thousands of failures. There's individuals out there that dedicated more time and committed themselves to achieving a goal that is at the least, next to impossible. To this day I have never been able to decide if I was a failure or not when it comes to this game. I think that everyone in this life has their own definition to what success just might be. Careers are defined, how exactly? If a baseball player plays for three years, but gets a career ending injury, yet he hit .300 for a living, has he failed because he isn't going to have played for 20 years? Or is it a successful career he had because of the stats he accumulated? Regardless of the fallout and where he finds himself at today? Is a successful career measured by a person's career, or how they're remembered after they're gone? I think I had a successful failure in the end. When it all ended, I had nothing left but a nice watch from Italy and a large debt with a line up a mile long that I had to take care of. To this day I still get reminded who I was and the things that I did. One way or the other I either get recognized in a casino or at a charity night. It still hasn't ended and I don't think that it ever will either. It's not that I am cursed, but it was a valuable portion of my life. Even with the negatives to come, I will always be proud of the risks I decided to act upon.

I have the upright most respect for poker players and gamblers alike. The hard part is that by the time the general public gets ahold of the view of a poker player, they see the final six players at a final table and everyone is so happy and guaranteed hundreds of thousands of dollars, if not millions. And life is great. They don't have a chance of seeing the pure exhaustion that it took for them to get to that destination. The levels and tribulations they had to go through to put up such a tremendous buy-in while all along making sure that every hand went the way they wanted it to. Or the amount of traveling it took for them to get to that point in their career also. All they see is a happy face, cash and instant fame on national television. That image can definitely make any normal human being that doesn't have the knowledge of the game, convinced that it looks like a simple life. In reality though, I would never wish upon anyone what I went through and what the true grinders go through on a daily basis.

I am going to try and remember as much as possible in the chapters to come. I feel, like I previously stated, that I have attempted to write this book a million times. But it seems like this is finally the most applicable moment to put all of this on paper and you'll eventually find out why. When all of this is finished, I'll finally have found peace with myself about a life I once lived somehow. Or so I wish. It was a life that to me doesn't make sense anymore in current thought. None of it really adds up and I have a hard time registering all of it in my mind after a million hours of reconciliation.

But all gamblers have a story, here's mine.

"The two most important days in your life are the day you are born and then the day when you find out why."

The Beginning-

"How did you first get started with poker?"

I used to hate this question to be honest. I have given countless of interviews and somehow this question always naturally came up.

There were so many new players in the game because of the poker boom in 2003 that it was simple to pinpoint and recognize immediately who had talent and who didn't. The guys that tried too hard were so exhausting to watch. They took the characters that they saw fresh off of ESPN and tried to mirror that image of them to the third degree. The sunglasses, headphones and hoodie characters who thought they knew everything about the game were the most annoying players to play against. They always had to talk about every hand, or bring up a bad beat from last week. And somehow, always, I ended up sitting next to them. They were mainly only in NL cash games or tournaments. Thankfully for me, I spent most of my time playing high stakes limit games and these types of players were nowhere to be found.

You would think that by the 100th time I gave an interview, I would have the answer down pat. I never really did to be honest. I would change my stories and stutter. Or actually want to ask them if they did any homework on me. You're interviewing me for a reason, so don't you know who I am? But my career went from small $1/$2 NL games in the distant Chicago suburbs, to the highest stakes Vegas had to offer on the drop of a dime. Both in the poker room and in the pits. A lot of things were still very new to me. I became numb to things very quickly because I was being put in situations so frequently that it didn't bother me anymore. Regardless of my inexperience and lack of a healthy lifestyle, I definitely became more accustomed to everything as time progressed. Just as any human would in any other day to day situation.

I knew I wanted to fly. Or be an astronaut. Just like any ordinary child, I wanted to be a professional athlete. Baseball was my sport of choice to be exact. You see these guys on baseball cards or on T.V. and then go to the stadiums with your dad and see thousands of people cheering them on, it was inspiring. And they made a ton of cash. Who wouldn't want that life, right? I definitely fell in love with flight. Something about just being so high up in the air and going hundreds of miles per hour intrigued me in ways I love until this very day. It definitely didn't help when my father was the only person in the neighborhood with surround sound and he would make my alarm clock the first five minutes to the movie "Top Gun." If anyone is not sure what those first few minutes are like, I simply feel sorry for you. To this day I still listen to a few songs from that movie as motivation. It definitely has changed my life for the better. My point is, is that we all have dreams as a kid. We all establish something that we want to be. Because in reality, that's what all of the adults around us are trained to do. All of the parents, teachers and coaches we have had in our past have definitely asked us what we want to do with the rest of our lives. It's just naturally in their psyche at that point to present those questions to us. Which in the end is completely acceptable, but it's not as well. Here are these mature adults with a career established out in front of them. They can direct us in any direction they want to. Don't they know that any kid at that age has absolutely no idea what the definition to life is? Or what they want to do? I mean, I know that we have to go through certain things in life to get to that next step that we want to be at. But still, I would have loved to have some counselor pull me aside and just tell me how it really is.

"Look, I'll be honest with you. All of this is bullshit. What you want now, is a far fetch from what you may want in ten years. Or even by the end of your first year in college or even after you graduate. Want to know why? People change and life evolves, simply no other way to put it. It doesn't mean that it's a bad thing either. That's just how life is. People make decisions and pull back on them based off of the experiences they have encountered while practicing that path. It is very difficult to say that you want to do something and make it a full commitment at 18 years old and in your first year of college. And then you're among the negatives and temptations of being at a college too."

Which honestly, are even more difficult than some of the life lessons I have ever been through. College is extremely difficult, on so many levels. And I didn't even finish. But I will get to that later on. I would have loved it if some counselor was just more honest with me on life than the way that they were. I understand that they need to be professional and uphold a certain persona to call it a day. Still, being realistic and honest is sometimes the best education some people can ask for in return. At the same time, it's up to us to make those goals and strive for them and maybe fail. Failure is in some way a giant key to success in this world. It makes you want it more and strive for that final dream down the road.

I definitely find it a good origin to train kids at such a young age to want and crave for some type of passion. Having passion in what you do in life is such an important necessity to have and to live by. If you establish and acquire that enough, they'll use it to their own knowledge down the road and who knows where that can take them. I definitely encourage that support. But yes, I had dreams as a kid. I blame those dreams for wanting such extravagant things, to the depth I took my poker career. Even to this day, and that is something I will probably say a lot in this book, but to this day I could never understand where I established such a detailed and over the top obsessions with everything that I did for the whole lifestyle I became a part of. That if I was going to do something, well then I had to be the best at it. I mean, why are you going to wake up every day of your life and not want to give it your all? I mean sure, when I am buying groceries I am not trying to be the best grocery shopper of all time. But with the things that can pinpoint and determine and checkmate your life, why not give it everything you have? I wish more people in life wanted to wake up every day and act like they were giving it their all. You get one shot in this life. Why not make it worth your while? Society would just naturally be a better place. But, I am neither the Commander in Chief nor some priest. So proceed as you will.

I have always tried to figure out where I became obsessed with numbers. I don't think I have ever found a solution. I used to cut off my second grade teachers with long division answers. To the point where they had to pull out calculators for confirmation of what they thought was obviously an incorrect answer. But I was always right. That list goes on of standout moments where I impressed myself. When I was about eight years old I want to say, Super Nintendo and regular Nintendo basically had a selection in their sports games where you could watch the computer play against itself entirely. You had the full option of selecting which teams were going to play each other and everything. At the early age of eight years old, I busted out the metric ruler sticks and made my own score sheets. I would put the teams into their own divisions and keep track of all of the player's stats. I would make up fake newsletters and have complete seasons. There would sometimes be hundreds of used scorecards all over my bedroom. Ask my parents for confirmation if you please. But, it was my little thing that I did. To this day I'm still very impressed by all of it.

That had to of been the introduction of my obsession for things. I would bring the scorecards to school and update my stats during lunch and when I had a few minutes at the end of my classes. At the same time, I was doing nothing but playing with numbers at all times. At an early age I was training my brain in different ways than other kids. I was constantly analyzing and somehow established that numbers existed in everything that we do in life. For some reason I thought that it was going to be an important ingredient in my life down the road. And it has been.

High school was an abundant four years. I can still admit that ten years later after it ended. I played baseball all four years and won two state championships. I was good in the offseason with the traveling teams I was a part of, but for whatever reason I locked up when I was on the diamond in my high school jersey with my teammates. I can never explain it to this day. I was two different players back then between the two elements I played in. I didn't grow up in the rich part of the district and most of these guys had known each other since they were in the Pony leagues. So there was definitely an association already previously established that I needed to find my way into. But, baseball was a great experience either way and I wouldn't have had it any other way to be honest.

They were a great group of guys and I would love to have a beer with any one of them to this very day. In the end, that's all a guy can ask for, right?

I was an asshole. I never applied myself when it came to academics. I don't know if it was laziness or thinking that down the path in life I would always find some way out and be successful. Don't get me wrong, I would have loved to have gotten straight A's. But, I was a regular B average student. I was a simple guy, ok with simple results.

I had acne, really bad acne. It was honestly one of the most difficult times in my life. I would wake up in the mornings and just cry my eyes out before I went to school. I couldn't find a solution to make it go away. I tried tons of medications. Some of them I reacted to and was allergic to and it just made it worse. Right around junior year, it started to disappear and it made the latter part of my high school career much more enjoyable. Some people were assholes and some weren't. Any kid at that age is still just a kid. So many more things to learn and maturity to obviously establish, that I kind of had what was coming to me.

I wore my heart on my sleeve. And I still do. I figured that there wasn't any other way to be. Maybe that's just because I had such intimate conversations with my father at such an early age. Pretty much about any topic and every reality situation you can ever imagine. My father had always been such an open book to life and its teachings, that I just naturally acquired some type of exposure to just always say what I felt met appropriate. Love is such an important factor in life. It defines so many questions that can lay unanswered unless it's experienced. Love is such an amazing feeling to be there in the moment and safe with someone else. A partner that you can't stand being without them for a single second of your day, regardless of anything that is going on in your life. That's one of the true searches in life. He always tried to make a connection with love and everything else. What I was getting at is that when that opportunity arose in high school, I gave it my all. I fell for pretty much two girls in high school. I had plenty of crushes, but these two will always stand out. So yes, I had my high school sweetheart. She will always be just that. A person defined in my past that will always mean the world to me.

I remember the first time I asked my mother for $20, I think. I had a job in high school for a month until I got fired. Like, seriously. Who the fuck fires a 15 year old kid? But, I was an idiot. Maybe someday I will explain why all of that drama went down. I feel like I have already told the story too many times. She threw me a $20 bill and I walked out. My buddy Matt had a gorgeous home by our school and a perfect finished basement. He was a quiet red headed kid, but extremely talented in certain things. We started playing random stupid card games in his basement. $20 buy-ins and we would divide the chips accordingly. I remember that we used to get excited when there was over $300 in the bank that lied on the floor. Fun games that I wish I could play today. King little, suicide, and screw the dealer. You know, back in the day when $5 was a lot of money and shit. That was definitely the formation of everything that I am about to explain.

All of us became addicted to it. We started playing 4-5 times a week. We were all best friends, so we were never trying to take each other's money in the end. We would borrow it back or give it back to each other. We were all close, but at the same time we were all very curious about No Limit Texas Hold em'. If we weren't sitting around playing, we were watching the World Series of Poker on ESPN, or putting on *Rounders* on repeat while we played tournaments together and taking it all in. Everything about our lifestyle became equipped with playing poker. It was sexy and intriguing and was blowing up all over the world quickly. We started playing in class, like literally during the middle of the teacher teaching us lessons. We would bust out a deck of cards anywhere we could and play the game. Gambling was definitely living up to its name, an addiction.

We got around to start ditching out the regular $20 buy-ins and we would buy-in for triple that or $100 and play .25/.50 No Limit cash games. Or we started playing tournaments. Depended on whatever crowd formed that night really. I had a huge group of friends back then that enjoyed playing cards. Some were serious about it and knew how to talk the language of the game, others didn't give a shit or have a clue and it didn't make any difference to them. Either way, I loved them all. They were my boys and we always had a good time. Those are the cherished times that I miss now. Just sitting around with your best friends, having some beers and no worries in life because you don't know what the real world is like just yet. Life is just kind of perfect with no setbacks.

Tournaments became our new thing. It was a way to win a lot of money, draw out the day and wasn't too expensive. Plus, if you busted out, cash games could always start up on the side. We played all different sorts. Sometimes we would get 40 guys together, or sometimes just 10. Buy-ins ranged from $20 to $100. But, I started to win all of them, literally. The game just clicked with me and I was starting to gain respect from that of my peers. And I was building a small bankroll if you wanted to call it that. Even though at that point in time I didn't even really know what a bankroll was, but it was still happening one way or the other.

High school carried on. We never stopped playing poker. It was our group of guys and we were always together. We switched it up and did random things during the day. We would play a lot of whiffle ball or home run derby. At night it always consisted of buying some beers and playing poker. Was something about the fact that we were all 18 years old and we were gambling just like we were those studs on ESPN. But, I knew that one day I would get there. I had visions and thoughts of just insane success with this game. I wanted to know what Vegas smelled like and I wanted to know how hot the desert was in the middle of summer. It sucked to think that I would have to wait another three years to get there. I wanted it now, right now in new ways that were all coming to me one by one. The more money I won, the higher the stake that I wanted to play. Except none of my friends wanted to move up in that price range, so I kept where I was at for now. I perfected the game with the tools that were provided to me. Since it was all I had at that current moment of time, I had to be perfect at it. I was constantly learning the game. It was a game that I was falling completely in love with and meant the world to me.

"The weight of being successful was replaced by the precision of being a beginner again, less sure about everything. It freed me to enter one of the most imaginative periods of my life."

Adaption-

I was looking forward to college. I would be lying if I didn't admit that. It was time for me to finally go away and be at a distance from my parents. They were my best friends and still are to this day, but it was time I took a step in whatever direction I was going to lead my life in. I was prepared for that transition. I knew that gambling was in the back of my mind because of the last 12 months of this new talent I had entrenched with my high school friends. I didn't stop thinking about it. I was getting so many positive feedbacks from my friends on different levels of how good I was, that I felt it to be a necessity to act upon whatever the game was advertising for me and my future. Maybe it was those comments and the motivation that they gave me that drove me early on in my career. Those statements gave me an early release to test myself. I guess in the end it was a mixture of ingredients that conducted my confidence to such a delicate prediction of what my life could possibly become. Only because it meant that much to me at such an early stage, had it become that important to me. Day in and day out, I was mentally gambling. I was assorting and assessing hands one after the other in my head. Just naturally I craved the game more and more each day.

We arrived at Lewis University in two cars and all of my shit cramped up tight in both vehicles. It upsets me today that I can't really remember the drive there or pulling in to the campus. I remember checking in and not really knowing what to do next. Sure I had to get all of my crap into my room. But this was a serious deal man. I was going to college and in a reality quick second thought I didn't know what the hell I wanted to do with my life. Subconsciously, I just wanted to gamble the entire time. Money was driving me into directions that I couldn't even really comply with. They were all new roads to me that I was a virgin to. I had to try and veer off to the acceptance path and try my best to get an education. I knew how important it was to my parents and just to the immediate demanding request of life. You have to get an education everyone told me, it's imperative. There's just simply no way that you can survive life without it. So yes, that scared me. Because a big part of me just knew that college wasn't going to work out in the end. I will admit now that I didn't have any drive to keep on going to school. That inner feeling I established definitely bothered me and I didn't see how any ounce of gambling would make me change that thought process. At the same time I was 18 years old and confused as fuck. Just like the rest of them. I look at it like this, if you truly know what you want to do with the rest of your life at such a young and stupid age, somewhere along the way you have been thoroughly brainwashed. There are still so many more life experiences that lay ahead of you to make such a definitive decision. But, I knew I had a talent in poker. I knew that my parents would be against it. But, I didn't have any other choice at that age other than to just wake up every day and see which lifestyle overcame the other.

Oh and another thing, I was on the baseball team too. So I had other obligations that I had to meet and dedicate myself to every day. The gym and early practices, the list went on. I didn't even want to play college ball to be honest. My father wanted me to and I knew how much it meant to him so I couldn't tell him no at that point. I spent a lot of time going 65 miles per hour. Whether it was me on the highways coming back from a private game at 3am before our 4am practices, or us just simply driving all over the Midwest in a traveling bus for away games. I was an exhausted individual at a very young age for a career that I didn't even knew existed at that point. With experience and everything that comes along with it, I gained that understanding.
College was something that I don't necessarily regret, but today I wish I was able to do both.

Realistically, it would have been impossible to do
the more I have thought about it. I was traveling and
gambling more sometimes than the amount of time I
was spending in class. I guess that can give you an
insight to how things were going for me back then.
Would I like to say today that I have a college
education, yes of course who wouldn't? It has
definitely made for some awkward conversations in
my past because it seems like everyone these days
has that accomplishment on their resume. Then they
ask why I don't and honestly, there is absolutely no
easy way for me to explain my past. Or even in a
short version. It becomes this long dialogue that in
the end the opposing person is just dumbfounded,
confused and finds their thoughts unable to give you
a response at the current moment in time. For
whatever reason I got used to it. It was much easier
to coordinate with strangers at airports or at the
poker table, than with friends I had known for a
lifetime. Some people understood it, others didn't. I
for whatever reason got used to explaining it in
more ways than one.

Baseball season started and I was probably the
worst player on the team. I didn't throw hard
enough and I was facing an injury that I didn't want
to deal with. I had an enflamed shoulder that was
getting worse by the day and I was doing nothing to
survive it. I think that is another thing that upsets
me about college. I kind of sort of just gave up with
baseball and my grades. Baseball definitely meant
the world to me, but for the level I was at, I knew
that I didn't stand a chance. Those guys threw hard
and I was barely breaking 82 miles per hour as a
righty. Which isn't that fast of a speed in Division II
baseball for the college level. I will admit this here,

that I only did any of that for my father, bottom line. I am not saying by any means that my life would have been different if I had a different freshman experience. But life could definitely be black and white as to what it is now. That's just a life experience that we all have to go through to get to the next one.

I told my father that I wasn't going to come back to the team sophomore year. That last game of the year against Iowa State was a very difficult moment for me. It was the only game all year long that we had a walk off win. It was the perfect culmination to my career in baseball. I remembered my first game in T-Ball, or the fact that my last at bat was a homerun just that previous summer. Or it was more than just that. It was the moments that I had and the opportunities that I had to be on that diamond with my dad and my teammates over the years. Whether he was my coach or not to be honest, doesn't change the fact that it was an important part of my life. Other than the games on the road in college throughout the midwest, I think my father missed two games in my entire life. That was when I was in T-Ball when I was 6 years old. He was there for everything after that. He always had an opinion after every game was finished too. So having to tell him that I am done with whatever career I had experienced, was extremely difficult for me. It was definitely a chapter in my life that I had to close with whatever type of closure I could grasp; in order for me to begin a career in something that I just simply felt had much more potential for my future.

Gambling, it has no definitive future. The next card that comes up is just as easily guessed as the floor man monitoring the area. It's completely undetermined, but that's just simply the risk that you are willing to take if you choose to accept that path. It becomes a part of you and sometimes even the money wasn't enough back then.

We had something in our area called the Charity Games. The CG gave under aged gamblers the ability to come into their casino nights and gamble. Because all of the proceeds they were accumulating, were going towards charity organizations all over the Chicago land area. So, at the early age of 18 I was going to local casino nights that were held in banquet halls and VFW's and playing live poker about 3-4x a week. They offered great tournaments, one table tournaments and cash games. Basically all of the elements that an up and coming gambler could dream of without being 21 years old. The CG became a huge part of my life and still is to this very day. I still know a lot of those guys and they're like brothers to me and always will be too.

The only balance that I ever accumulated in those few years in my life that I was a professional poker player, was that I was the best poker dealer in Chicago. Trust me I have plenty of witnesses that can approve of that statement. Even when I would win $50k a week in Vegas or anywhere in the country, I would still show up to deal at high stakes games in the underground world of Chicago. This was my lifestyle. I couldn't just go and have a part time job somewhere and act like I was living a normal life. I needed to stay within the element I had become a part of. Because when I was dealing poker, I was able to watch the game. Even though I was still playing stakes sometimes 10x or 20x the amount I was dealing, there was still a game that was developing in front of me. Poker is all about a pattern really. It doesn't matter what stake you're dealing, it's all the same game really. If you can accept that and understand that, you can definitely implement that into your everyday poker career. So yes, I dealt cards. Yes I was awesome at it and I still have that hidden talent inside of me. It's like riding a bike to me really. You could throw me in a $25/$50 Pot Limit Omaha Hi/Lo game right now, and I wouldn't skip a beat. Because that love and those moments of accomplishments were so special to me, that they will never leave my conscious.

When sophomore year had started, I felt like I wasting my time. I will explain later on about my internet winnings, but mixed in with dealing and CG, I had about $60k to my name. That is a ton of cash to a 19 year old kid. I promise I still didn't know which direction that I wanted to go though. I wanted to continue to strive in my college career. I wanted to make my parents happy in the end. I promise you that was my intention. I knew how much it meant to them and with that, it meant a lot to me to make them happy. But, I had this hidden talent, that wasn't so hidden anymore. I started to get recognized much more at CG events and what not. I went on a streak where I won their nightly tournament of 100+ players five times in a row. In less than a week I had won $20k or so and didn't know what to do with myself. Around campus word got out what I was doing on my off time and that I had a lot of cash. With that, I lived at home sophomore year. I only lived a few minutes from school. I felt that it would be the smartest course to not be on campus as much. People do stupid things and I am completely blessed that I only had a gun pointed at my face twice in the duration that I did what I did. Given the stature I was at and the element of situations that I put myself in, I should definitely be dead right now to be honest. How I survived any of this is beyond me.

Here was the thing, on the weekends CG would go up to Rockford, IL for their events. So, since baseball was no longer a part of my life and taking up my weekends, I started to go up to Rockford by myself. The manager of CG ran a house game at his place on Friday's that I dealt at and I would sleep on his couch when the game finished up in the early hours of the morning. Then we would have events on Saturday and Sunday. I would simply just deal three days every weekend. I came home Monday mornings at the early hours of the morning completely exhausted back to my house, but the money was worth it. All of it definitely was taking a toll on me though. I was making $1k-$1,500 a week and I was 19 years old. At the same time, trying to go to class accordingly without being too tired, definitely became my biggest road block at that point in my life.

Word began to get out in the poker world just who I was and the type of talent and knowledge that I had accumulated at such a young age. Not just the establishment I made as a player, but that I was the best in both attributes of the game. Whether it was dealing or playing. With that, definitely became more opportunities within the area. Because of the poker boom, there was a house game in every county on every day of the week. Somehow I became established with all of them. I could play in the game, but the stakes were so low that the money wasn't enough for me. It was weird because I would have no problem ever dealing all night long and making $300-$500. It was definitely a different type of feeling. I could show up to the games and play and have a great time and maybe make $500-$1k playing a night. It may have been the only time in my life where I would take the safe route in things and just made cash dealing because it was available. With that, it made me never say no to dealing cards, ever. Like I said before it gave me the ability to be around the game and to practice it and make some good cash. Even though I had money, it was still meaningful.

I believe it was the first game in the city that I had dealt at. It was a private Italian club on the west side of Chicago. It had security cameras and bodyguards, gorgeous waitresses and some of the best players from the city. There I was at 19 years old, controlling the game twice a week and making about $40/hr. I was shuffling and shipping pots worth thousands of dollars to these guys. A $5/$10 NL game where everyone bought in for $1k. Which give it a few hours or so and there was all of a sudden $50k on the table. The game was enormous, not something I was used to. It definitely got me used to being around cash and that type of intensity. It was so cool because all of the guys were respectable individuals. Gentlemen that in the long run I would end up playing against and they would shake my hand after a huge hand because they never expected it from me, a guy they looked at as just a poker dealer and didn't know my background or capabilities. Then when that pot was dragged my way, I established that respect.

I was on break and I made a phone call to my father on a lonely night in the corner of one of the rooms, with the radio on behind me. I had no intentions on registering for my spring semester of sophomore year. Probably the biggest decision that I have made in my life up to this point, because I knew that it was going to affect everything from here on out. I don't think that I ever admitted to him that it was my mother's decision for me to leave school. I was vulnerable for some reason. In the beginning it was my mother's opinion to make me leave college. She saw that I was coming home at random hours of the morning and staying awake for 36 hours at a time and that my grades were awful. It was my mother that pretty much told me and asked me why I was doing this to myself. That the best decision was for me to leave Lewis and to attempt a chance at a poker career. She saw the type of money I was dealing with and the time and effort that I was putting towards it. When I finally told my father the news, I don't think we talked for a couple of weeks. I had about $100k at that point. $100k was plenty of cash for a 19 year old kid to have as a bankroll and to begin a real career. So I did. I think he ended the conversation by hanging up on me and I was devastated. It was something I had to expect and begin to deal with if I was going to make it work. I was in this on my own from here on out.

I spent most of my playing time on PartyPoker. It was the only internet site really back then that had the most action on it. I became satisfied with not playing live poker and only dealing live poker. I could play online anywhere that had an internet connection and it was convenient and fast paced as well. Plus, they offered thousands of tournaments a day and high stakes limit cash games. When I say high stakes at this point in my career, I mean anything from $20/$40 up to $100/$200. To this day I still say that the most skill in the game is involved in limit hold em, not NL. Sure, both games are unique in their own elements, but it takes a lot more skill to double your stack in limit than that of NL. You can play one hand a night in NL and make good. With limit poker you have to establish the talent and inner self trust that you have in your hand to make that necessary river bet. Because in the end, those entire river bets add up to a lot of dough by the end of the night. And if you don't have that knowledge secured somewhere in your gut instincts, you're missing out on a lot of money at the end of the year.

PartyPoker became extremely addicting. What else did I expect was going to happen? I became overly obsessed with the game and was given the ability to see thousands of hands a day as opposed to maybe a few hundred if I was playing live. I would play online during the day and deal at random house games at night. I was making about $2k a week guaranteed from dealing. I spent a lot of time playing at friend's houses because my mother ran her own business out of her home and I didn't want to disrupt something that she had been building for 30 years. Most of my time was spent on a random laptop somewhere cooped up and focusing on improving my game each and every day, which gave me the early development of fast paced action and degeneracy.

PP ran nightly "super tournaments" they called them. I think they were $162 buy-ins. Every Wednesday was a limit tournament. The first two that I played I won both of them. Pocketing about $20k for each tournament and boosting my bankroll

to right around $150k just weeks after making that
demoralizing phone call to my father. I wanted to
share these accomplishments with him, but I felt
like he would just simply not understand to be
honest. It was hard to brag about my
accomplishments to that of my friends and people I
had known since I was a kid. I didn't want to sound
like I was a psycho and was just making up stories
to try and impress people. I truly believe that a lot
of people did start to believe that everything I was
saying was nothing but a bundle of lies. Since all of
the stories I would tell them were so intense and out
of this world, that they were impossible to believe at
some points. I can't blame them either. If you read
this whole thing through, I am sure you will have
your own opinions too.

The first tournament that I ever won was that first
Super Wednesday Limit tournament on PP. There
were about 500 players in it and it made me
understand that tournaments were very profitable. I
just risked $162 and won $19k. More than 130x
return on my investment or ROI for all of you
intelligent individuals out there. With tournaments
brings on a whole different lifestyle than the one I
was used to playing high stakes cash games. You
could play for hours upon hours in a tournament,
days sometimes, and walk away with nothing. Or in
cash games I could play for a couple of hours and
win thousands and call it a day. It was extremely
gratifying and meaningful winning that first
tournament in 2005, but I didn't know what to make
of it. I was overwhelmed. Sure I was making good
money dealing and playing the stakes I did every
day, but that was my biggest score up to that date. A
boost of confidence is never an atrocious thing for

anyone. Over the next week I played cash games and leading up to the following Wednesday I figured it was only proper to play in the same tournament again. Even though the possibility of winning back to back tournaments of the same stature seemed next to impossible, I figured why not.

When I reached the final table again, I had plenty of rail birds watching me. Rail birds are just friends or foes that are rooting for you or against you and I also had about ten people standing behind me watch me play at my friend's house. Plus the chat box on the game's screen was blowing up with comments about me. I was a regular in the high stakes cash game tables and then I won the tournament the week before also, only to be back at the same final table again seven days later, it was exciting to watch and to be a part of. The final hand played out pretty standard for heads up limit. I two bet with pocket 8s, he three bet with A7, I four bet and he called. He was next to all in before the flop was dealt out and fittingly it popped up as 723 and we raised it until he got all of his chips in the middle. It panned out the Js and the Jh and that was it. I won the same tournament in back to back weeks and shot my bankroll up to right around $150k. It was a huge confidence booster for me again. With that came more attention and requests from friends that I wasn't ready to give into yet.

I had become a leader to some sort of degree and viewed as the best, especially after this second victory in such a short amount of time. That people started to ask me to borrow money or teach them how to play. It became a large responsibility at such a young age. I had come to know a lot of guys at my age that weren't as fortunate with money, but they were inspired by the game and were trying to become something of themselves. I felt like I had to help them out. But my biggest problem was sure, I have this cash, but I didn't understand the value of anything I was making. I was winning in such large sums, that I had no idea what $20 was or even $100. So it was easy for me to lend out money or to stake guys in games or tournaments. Sure, I dealt and got tipped $1 or more a hand, but I was just doing it to have some cash flow coming in and to be around the game. Plus, I was so natural and good at it that time just kind of flew by. I didn't really view it as work and when I got tipped, I got tipped in chips, not cash. This was all a start to me not understanding or appreciating what money was. Or how much that money truly meant in life. It did nothing but create a snowball effect that drove me into the ground by the end. But, every ending has a beginning. Playing on PP was definitely a good experience in regards to dealing with getting accustomed to high stakes games and what it takes to win tournaments. It was a good learning experience.

But, it was time to start traveling.

"To travel in this life is to live."

Shakopee-

I was at a house game one night just dealing like usual, and I shocked myself in the surprising fact that you didn't have to be 21 to gamble in some states. How I didn't know this information was beyond me. Regardless of my involvement in the CG, I thought you had to be 21 to gamble at any casino in the country. Turns out you don't and that excited me like no other knowing that I was going to be able to walk into a real casino, sit down and play poker with no worries about how old I was. I had gotten word of this through a close friend and began to investigate. Since I was a fan of high stakes limit hold em', I came to the conclusion that Canterbury, located just outside Minneapolis in a town called Shakopee, offered the best options. NL wasn't legal in their state for some reason and it was a short 56 minute flight from Chicago. This stage in my life is important, because traveling would become a huge factor in my life and poker career. It's a process and definitely a fundamental that is a necessity to a poker player's course of action. Packing, planning, getting to the airport, the process, arriving, cab to the hotel, checking in and getting situated and then hitting the tables and getting to work. This was going to be my first time experiencing all of that. Sure, I drove 90 minutes to Rockford every weekend for about a year straight, but flying somewhere for an occupation is gratifying and terrifying at the same time. I had zero idea what I was doing really and just had to take it all in as a new experience as it came to me and to go from there.

I had a few good dealing sessions and a couple good sessions online playing $30/$60 in the last couple of weeks. Plus, I had some genius contend me to playing a heads up live shootout for $3k. We played $50/$100 limit until one of us had it all and we called it quits. This wouldn't be the first time that he would challenge me to something of this degree either. Over the course of the next four years, he and I would play heads up shootouts 21 times. For buy-ins ranging from $1k to $10k, and in the end I would go 18-3. Of course the only times he beat me were for the $1k buy-ins. (Insert smiley face here).

Since $30/$60 was the largest limit Canterbury had to offer back then, I was only going to bring $10k with me. I figured that was enough for five buy-ins and simply if I lost that much playing a limit to that degree, I deserved to pack my bags and head back to Chicago. Now, up until this point the highest stakes I had played live were $2/$5 NL. There weren't any live limit games offered up to that point that I qualified for. All of my limit talent had been established online. Sure, I played what's his face a few times in shootouts, but that is completely different than sitting down at a table to a stake of that magnitude for the first time. It's an extremely high stake and lots of risk involved. But, I had to convince myself that I was ready. I had been playing some of the largest stakes the internet had to offer for a while now and was successful. I knew how much I loved live poker and I needed to take this gamble. Even if I lost, it would be an experience that needed to develop to give other doors the opportunity to open for my newly established career.

I made the decision the night before at the last second. I don't even think I told my mother until I was leaving that morning with a bag packed and ready to go as to where I was going. It was just a quick decision that it was time to go and see what this other life was all about. I was up before the sun rose and I drove to the airport as early as I could. I think my flight was at 8am and I got there around 6am. I had never traveled by myself before and was terrified and anxious and everything that came along with it. From the entrance that I walked in to Midway Airport, AirTran Airways was the first desk. I assumed that they would have the cheapest flights to Minneapolis. I was right, a large sum of $63 one way to Minneapolis. I felt like a God. I bought a one way ticket since I really had no prediction as to how long I would stay there. I packed enough clothes to last me a week and figured I could meet that complication when the time came if I needed to find some soap.

I didn't know what I was doing really. I was literally just a kid. I had just turned 20 years old and wasn't looking forward to another cold winter. But, Shakopee seemed like my next destination for now. It was located about 30 minutes outside of Minneapolis. An easy $50 cab ride to reach a week full of plenty of action.

It seemed like by the time I finished my Coke, we were already descending. There I was ready for anything and walking off a plane willing to meet whatever challenge was ahead of me. All of it was a brand new road in front of me. Literally every single step was going to be a brand new experience for me. I had one year to get ready for Vegas. Because trust me, the second I turned 21, my ass was going to be on a plane to the desert. Because that's where it's all at, the life of a gambler somehow always develops or dies in Vegas. I had to find out which one was going to be me. But again, I had another year to prepare for it. I thought Rockford and CG were the pure arrangement for that, but I looked at Canterbury as a full on opportunity to test myself to a standpoint I had yet practiced.

I walked outside in the freezing cold and grabbed a cab. All I had was my red Nike bag that was my traveling bag from Lewis' baseball team. It would become my closest entity the next few years of living in and out of airports and hotels. I jumped into the cab and told the driver, "Canterbury Casino please." He kind of turned around and looked at me like what the hell do you mean? But, I just smiled and stared out the window like a little kid. I just wanted to get there. I just wanted to walk into their poker room and be a face that no one knew. I wanted to earn their respect by beating them in ways they had never seen before. Just win 100 big bets a day and end the session. Then walk out like it was just a regular Tuesday to me. I had done this many of times on PP and was ready to make this a reality in live poker. With the money values of the chips staring me directly in the face, with having to make on point decisions that are going to further my future, I was finally in an element that I could get used to fulfilling that.

When I arrived on Canterbury's property, they had three hotels to choose from. I picked a random one and asked if they had any rooms available. They obliged and I figured I would ask for three nights for now. Figured that nothing too awful could happen in 72 hours and I can go from there based off of how I was doing. It was $37 a night and sounded worth it. I checked in, but it was only about 9:30am. I really didn't know if people played poker that early on in the day. So, I called the poker room and asked.

"Um, yes sir. We have two $30/$60 games going and three $15/$30 games too in case you want to play lower."

I said thanks and hung up the phone. Clearly I was completely uneducated or to even second guess a gambler's need at any given time of the day. I could see the casino from the front of the hotel, so I decided to take the fifteen minute walk, regardless of it being 20 degrees outside. I was bundled up enough where I was alright. The bricks of cash I had in my pockets provided me some type of warmth I had never experienced before.

I walked in and it wasn't exactly what I had expected. Canterbury was also a race track, so it wasn't the same type of casino you may be envisioning. It was more of an open banquet hall lined up with tables and a cage and pit area and then another huge open room for tournaments. But, I didn't really care. I was ready. I was first on the

$30/$60 list and waited for my name to be called. Not ten minutes went by and it was time to put everything I had learned and experienced these last couple of years, into play. Finally, it was my turn to see if I can do this. But, at the same time I couldn't take my result to this first live high stakes action as a documentation to what my career was projected to be either. Thankfully, I knew this already coming in. I had liked to think that even given my inexperience and young age, I was still very confident in my capabilities. I had already been playing the highest stakes in the world that the internet had to offer for over a year. I crushed those games like I was playing with play money. Bottom line is that I was demoralizing my opponents anywhere I played and I needed to get my shit together right away and play this game the way I knew how to play it. That is very important in anything that you do in life. Just sit down like you own the place and you'll be just fine. You can thank my father for that quote.

Before I knew it, eight hours had gone by. I was starving and the game was magical as anything I had ever dreamed of. The game was a three chip six chip concept. So obviously on the flop you would bet three chips indicating $30 and I would hope that you could figure out the rest. But the game was unreal. I remember I told myself that going into it that I wasn't going to be upset if I lost. It had been a while since I had a losing session, but I needed to go into this with an open mind. I needed to understand that for probably a little while, that all of these sessions were going to be learning experiences I needed to take in and capture. Whether I won or lost I needed to capture how I felt towards both scenarios and save them for later results as well.

The first session came and went. Before I knew it, it was midnight. I had just played a 14 hour session and I was up about $900. Which isn't a ton for $30/$60, but still I booked a win in my first ever live high stakes limit game. I walked back to my hotel extremely proud of myself on so many different levels. It's like it was my first game in the major leagues and I struck out the side and called it a day. I remembered that I couldn't sleep. And before I knew it, it was 5am and I wanted to go back to that same seat and do it all over again. Thankfully enough I fell asleep and definitely needed some rest. I had been up already for 24 hours and needed to regroup myself.

I ended up staying for four days on this trip and winning $4,300. I was getting an understanding as to what life was like on the road as a poker player. The random hours, breakfast for dinner and vice versa and of course, extremely lonely. Actually, any meal is available at any time of day for a poker player. But trust me I was nowhere near where I wanted to be. Minnesota was a great experience the first time around and over the next twelve months I would go back there another 14 times. I would love to explain in more details about it, but I could go on for 100 pages for what Canterbury meant to me and some stories about sessions I had. It taught me a piece of maturity about traveling and the responsibilities I needed to take on as a professional poker player at such a young and daring age. I began to know the floor men on a first name basis and even the regulars. I haven't been back there since I was 20 years old, but I am glad that I found an establishment that I could practice at before Vegas arrived. 14 trips back and forth, long hours grinding in the midst of an upcoming new and exciting career, left me happy when it was time for me to leave Canterbury. It was a profitable destination of about $80k in those trips.

When I wasn't in Minnesota, I had migrated to the highest staked games in the underground world of Chicago. A dark, intriguing and extremely dangerous place that even to this day, I can't believe I came out alive in. My bankroll was creeping up on $250k and I was ready to play higher stakes for the time that I was home in Chicago and not in Minnesota and just not yet 21 either. Canterbury was just the right amount of practice for me for what lied ahead. Word of mouth in the poker world travels quickly. I had been getting random invites to private games all over the city. With games ranging from $20/$40 all the way up to $25/$50 PLO and $400/$800 Mix. Which are just ridiculous limits to be playing when I think about it these days, but, I could afford it and I had never been more anxious in my life for an opportunity such as this. I knew I needed to work towards that challenge at the same time. I needed to treat this like a business as much as possible. So, if I wasn't in Minnesota I was in the city. Grinding in some of the most difficult and high stakes games the Midwest had to offer. And I was winning.

"The most dangerous creation of any society in the world is the man who has nothing to lose."

Underground World-

It was the beginning of 2006 when I finally started to get around to attending house games on a more daily basis. All of them were different. As for now, I stuck primarily off in the distant Chicago suburbs. Townhouses, houses, apartments, back rooms of auto repair shops. Really just anywhere you can find room to set up a poker table. I had exhausted myself with the internet really. I still had about $20k on PP, but I wasn't really using it much anymore. I had become some sort of a bank actually. Everyone knew I had funds up there and if they needed money I would send it to them and then they would hand me the cash. It was more of a security withholding if anything. I knew it was there if I ever needed anything. Plus, I would help out my friends with it too and what not. I was staking guys and lending out money left and right. I wanted to help out as many people as I possibly could and I clearly had a problem with saying no. To this day I wasn't positive where I accumulated that want or desire to make others happy. I loved picking up dinner tabs and just being there for people. Maybe because I knew they needed it. I was doing what I was doing and they were just college students at this point. Anyway, I had no value to the dollar since I was making so much. So it was nothing but a silent overwhelming experience.

I was playing so much more live poker that I felt more like a professional rather than some bum sitting at the computer all day long in sweats with headphones on. I loved the sounds of the chips clashing together and looking down at pocket aces or turning the nuts. And the best of it, stacking up your chips after winning hands. The list went on. I was becoming more accustomed and comfortable being at the table wherever I was. I have Canterbury to thank for that pleasure and establishment.

I started to attend a lot of the suburban games, probably five days a week. The other two days were pretty much restricted for sleep to be honest. These house games were magical. They would sometimes go on for days, 48 hours even and the players would just filter in and out as time went by. The lineups were interesting. Every occupation and age you can think of would fill those rooms. Anyone and everyone back then had the curiosity of what it was like to play poker and to be a poker player. It was such an appealing and curious game to millions all over the world and growing at a rapid rate too.

I met Jeff at a small game in Naperville he was running with a buddy of his for some extra cash. He was tied into the city games though and to this day he is one of the biggest degenerates I have ever known. He is the epitome of what not to do with money. He was just awful at handling it and holding onto it. He got a better high off losing his money at blackjack and baccarat than winning and cashing it out at the cage. That's the unexplained sickness to some gamblers. Some gamblers literally get a better feel of themselves when they watch the chips being taken away from them. Every once and a while he would go on little runs, winning $5k-$40k. But just like me back then, nothing was ever enough for our desires or what we craved. There is a reason why he was always dealing. But, he was dealing at these high stakes games in the city. Making $1k a night usually if the crowd was right or the game went on forever. Mixed in with his little game in the suburbs that ran three times a week, he had all the tools to be making $200k a year in cash. But, we all make decisions in life and 95% of his were down the wrong path.

Jeff and I got to talking one night when he decided to stick around for his game. Usually he would just drop off money to his partner if he needed it or bring the food and drinks on by before the game started and before he headed to the city. When it came to house games and even tournaments, I wasn't the kind of guy that would show up an hour late or halfway through the night. I wanted to

usually always be there when the game was starting.
I felt like I was always missing out on opportunities
if I wasn't there when the cards first went in the air.
I just viewed it that every hand was essential to the
growth of my young career. Jeff saw that I was a
different type of breed and had heard that I was
killing it at games up in Minnesota. Like I stated
before, you couldn't really just walk into most of
these city games. You had to know someone who
knew someone before you were allowed in. Jeff
knew everyone and dealt at two of the biggest limit
games in the city. I couldn't have really found a
better insight to the Chicago operation.

I came to realize that it became difficult to find high
stakes cash games in the city that were NL. Most of
the games were limit because that type of game
moved much faster which would favor the rake and
the house would make more money. Hands didn't
take as long, decisions were made quicker and it
was more difficult for players to go broke. In return
that helps the house out tremendously with not
having to do favors to keep the game moving along
or even having to sit down and keep the game alive.

He said that he had asked his bosses, the guys who
owned the games if I could be allowed to come and
play and they didn't see an issue with it. So, it was
about that time I ditched the suburban games and
moved up in the ranks to the city games. I had no
idea what to expect. We had been discussing what it
was like and that these players were true
professionals, cops, businessmen, lawyers, drug
dealers, athletes, list went on. He said sometimes
there are so many chips on the table that they would
have to start playing with cash too. The pots are just
enormous and the game moves incredibly quick and

is quite taxing. He knew I had played the biggest stakes online and $30/$60 up in Canterbury. But the way he made these city games sound like, fuck was I excited.

I was finally nervous about something. I don't think I ever got nervous heading to a poker game. Maybe it was a good thing knowing I was testing myself to degrees that frightened even my psyche. The feelings I accumulated from going to Canterbury or the suburban games was more on the excitement and anticipation side. I was young and winning and I had no reason to not be as confident as I was. For whatever reason this time around, I was sweating and anxious as shit to finally get down there. The games were highly illegal and if my guesses were correct, there was always over $100k in the room, minimum. Between what was on the table and whatever was in our pockets. It was an intimidating atmosphere sometimes. If I was going to be playing in these games and the level that I felt like I was ready to be a part of, I needed to shove that fear aside and just play the game I loved with passion and an open mind. Whatever element I was putting myself into. Do I think they were the correct decisions today? I'm still alive so I guess they were.

The first game that I was going to was the "Grand & Damen" game. It was located at that intersection on the west side of Chicago, roughly half a mile north of the United Center. When I got the directions from Jeff, I was scared about the area being unsafe. Growing up I remembered all of the times I went to the city with my father and he used to always tell me to never go in that vicinity around the UC. It was filled with the projects and gangs and there was just no reason I needed to put myself in that position. I was driving a bright red Jeep Wrangler that was covered in chrome and could be noticed anywhere on the road. I didn't want to become an easy target to whoever wanted to make a bad decision on the wrong night. Not to mention that I had $10k in my pocket all the time.

I got off at the Damen exit off I-290 and headed north. It was just a few minutes until I got to Grand avenue and found a parking spot. The street was a busy one, but there wasn't any traffic anywhere. The building was three stories tall and had two entrance doors. I could barely read the address. I gave Jeff a call and he told me he would buzz me in. I got out of my car and waited for the buzz. It went off and I walked in. In front of me was a staircase with at least 20 steps to the first floor. What must have been 40 feet above me until I finally found the ceiling too. I walked up and was greeted by bodyguards and surveillance cameras. They patted me down for safety reasons and I began to look around. It was a two story loft with cathedral ceilings and an open floor plan. The walls were brick and the kitchen appliances were steel. The wooden floor boards looked like they were polished for days before the start of the game. There were TVs everywhere, beautiful waitresses and two tables capacitated with players. I didn't know a single player and you could tell that I was getting a look of confusion by all the players there as to who I was. I spotted Jeff and was greeted by Brian, the owner. He was a short Italian guy who had a cocaine problem and always seemed to be the happiest guy in the world. He had tan skin and slicked back black hair packed with gel and he was always walking around in slippers. He ran this game four times a week and was making upwards of about $500k a year from it. But, with a heavy coke problem and video poker addiction, he was just trying to stay afloat.

Both games were full, but it sounded like a couple of players were leaving pretty soon. The waitress, who was possibly the most gorgeous girl I had seen up to that point in life, put her hand on my back and asked me if I wanted anything to drink while I waited. Now, at that point I wasn't an alcoholic. So I am sure I asked for a soda and went from there. These games also had anything you wanted when it came to drinks or food. If they didn't have it, they would go and get it for you. They were making so much money that there wasn't any other choice. The bodyguards were huge. Dressed all in black, with guns in their holsters, each one was about 6'7 and 350 pounds. But, they ended up being close friends of mine as time would pass and both of them were just big teddy bears.

"Seat open."

Both games were $40/$80 with a $50/$100 kill. A kill game was if a player won two hands in a row with at least seeing a flop, the limits would go up. As long as the same player kept winning, the kill pot stayed in rotation. It was just a nice way to increase action without boosting the limits entirely. If you're wondering what my longest streak was of kill pots, it was in this game a few months later when I won 11 hands in a row when we were four handed. Think I won about $6,500 that night.

I finally sat down and bought in for $2k. The chips were in increments of $10 even though they weren't marked. So it was a four chip/eight chip game. Which made it easier for the dealers and convenience for the speed of the game by having less chips in play. But still, some guys had thousands in front of them and it was hard to even see the surface of the table on some days.

I was playing pretty tight the first couple of hours and folding hands to raises that I don't think I would've folded if I was sitting in the same seat at Canterbury. I understand now that you need to make some type of an establishment in anything you do in life. I think I was just looking for that moment in time where I felt it was correct. And it came.

I was under the gun with 8s7s. For anyone reading this that doesn't read much about poker, that means the 87 of spades. The "s" symbolizes spades. So going forward, if it says 8d7d, that means diamonds, 8h7h means hearts and 8c7c means clubs. Just for future reference.

My first hand I ever played in the game I two bet under the gun with 8s7s to $80. I got three bet to $120 and the button four bet to $160, I called and the original guy who raised me five bet and capped it at $200. The flop panned out beautifully for me, 6sKs5c. I flopped an open ended straight flush draw. I led out for $40, got two bet and three bet by the time it came back to me and I four bet it, only to have the original guy who raised me cap it at $200 apiece. There was already $1,200 sitting in the middle of the table with two cards to come. The turn was an offset 2h and I completely missed any of my outs. I checked and the guy to my left bet $80 only to get raised by the guy on the button to $160.

I called and so did the guy to my left. The river was the most beautiful card in the deck, the 4h. The river gave me the straight and I had what is known as the nuts. The nuts were defined as the best hand possible, not another hand could beat it. I led out on the river and got called by both players and flipped over the hand like it was just any other hand at Canterbury. Felt like it all happened in slow motion and everyone was shocked that I was holding the hand that I was. I had beaten AK and a set of kings. I dragged in the $2k pot and tipped the dealer $15 and started stacking my chips, already up $1,300 or so. All it takes sometimes is that one hand to get you settled in and comfortable. I began to notice the other players giving me that look of acceptance. In return, it was important for me to have that respect anywhere I was. I didn't want to just be some other player at the table taking up space, I wanted them to know that I was trying to become the best player they had ever seen.

By the time that night had finally ended for me, right around 6am and nine hours later, I was up $4,800. As the game went on and guys either left or others made more money, the limits always went up. When I left we were playing $80/$160. So the game had doubled throughout the course of the night. I shook Brian's hand and he told me I could come back any time that I wanted to. The game ran four times a week. By the time I made the hour ride home, which was really the only exhausting process of it all, went to sleep and woke up again, there was another game that was going to begin shortly. I had no problem coming home after a long session and easily sleeping for 12-16 hours at a time. Plus, it's always easier to sleep after a winning session.

Always had to take a long hot shower when I got home just to get the filth of it all off of me, mixed with the smoke, constant contact of the tables and chips, I was filled with grime after every session.

Drugs were everywhere down there. Mostly marijuana and cocaine was the drug being passed around the room. Sometimes you could go in the bathroom to take a piss and the top of the toilet looked like someone dumped flour onto it. They would take turns going into the bathroom and taking hits. I can appreciate the fact that I never did any of it and stayed clean even with the temptations I was given every day.

The Grand & Damen game was a memorable place for me. A place that I will always remember and hold it close to me and the success I had in the game. It really helped me become someone in the city. I was making a name for myself. I was establishing respect in all parts and grounds I could walk onto, which made the long sessions I was playing, more gratifying. Nothing about what I was doing was relaxing or easy. If I treated it that way, I could become complacent and veer down the wrong path very quickly. I still treated every session as challenging as I could. I tried to figure out who the best player was in each game and make sure I beat him so bad that everyone knew why I was starting to be called the best in Chicago. But I didn't really feel that way. I didn't want them to think that I was thinking it either. I didn't want them to see some 20 year old kid dominating the game at such a young age and with the amount of cash I had as a bad person based on lack of experience. I wanted them to know that I was among them. Not below them or above them. I just had so much heart for this game, and it showed with my winning sessions.

Over the course of the next ten months, I would go back and forth from the Grand & Damen game to the Chinatown game and many others too. I definitely left a dent in the Grand & Damen game. I beat up some games so bad that to this day I haven't seen anyone beat limit games the way that I used to. Normal players would win $1k-$2k and call it a day. I would put the hours and time in and sometimes win $6k-$10k. Playing sometimes for 36 hours straight, sleeping upstairs in the spare bedroom and showering and coming back downstairs and starting all over again. It never ended really. This was the career I chose and I needed to make sure that I was putting forth the effort to better myself every day. Regardless if I was conducting winning streaks that would last months at a time, I was still trying to treat it as a progressing education of my own. I was still learning new things every day based off of situations and hands I was experiencing. In the end, I couldn't have asked for a better experience there.

About three years later in 2009, the game died out. Brian had overdosed on cocaine and was in the hospital for a while. Since he didn't really have a partner with the game, it disappeared. I heard a few years later that he had sobered up and was a bartender at a hot club in the city. I couldn't be more proud of him. He was kind of like a big brother to me. He always gave me anything I ever asked for and was always watching out for me on a lot of different levels. He would motivate me and always make time to chat. I never looked down on him for his coke problem, because that part of him didn't bother me. We looked past the cash and what we were doing for a living and we were always honest with each other. Great guy and I hope that today he is alive and well.

Every once and a while I find myself crossing that intersection these days and I can't help but give that building a look just to see if it's still there. Last time I drove past it, it still had a for rent sign in the window. Now it's just filled with empty floor plans and ghostly images of some of the best moments in my career.

Just a few miles east, the "Skyscraper" game was a big step in my career. I started playing in it in the summer of 2006. It was the highest stakes game I had ever seen that was not in a casino. It was a $200/$400 mix game. Which usually started out as just regular limit hold em, but as more players sat down, it primarily became an incredible H.O.R.S.E game. Which is an acronym for Hold em, Omaha Eight or Better, Razz, Stud Hi and Stud Eight or Better. Sometimes though, we would throw in a few more games and before we knew it we were playing 10-12 games at once based off of a rotation. So whenever the button got back to the one seat, the game would switch. Popular other games were Badugi, 2-7 Triple Draw and Pineapple to name a few.

The money didn't bother me really. I was comfortable sitting down in a game of that magnitude and buying in for $10k and seeing where it took me. My bankroll was right around $310k at this point. I was only risking 3%-5% of everything I had, which was a good bargain given the limits I was playing. Pretty much soaking off of the confidence I had already accumulated up to this moment in my career. It didn't take me more than winning one hand in a new game to calm my fears and let my psyche and talent take over like a machine. Then I was home free. I got into the Skyscraper game from a guy I met at the Grand & Damen game. That was one of the most interesting things about the city games in that each game had its own nickname. The Skyscraper game was nestled in one of Chicago's tallest buildings on the 57th floor. The game was tucked away in the corner of an apartment worth close to $2 million. Equipped with any luxury you could think of such as floor to ceiling windows, gorgeous waitresses, Chicago cops as security and a view of the city to die for. The guy that ran the game, his name was Tyler and he worked at the Chicago Board of Trade and loved to gamble. Mainly on sports, but enjoyed poker. He rarely played though. Aside from the poker game that he ran once a week, he was a bookie to a client list of about 50 guys. All betting different sports and he would never take a bet lower than $1k. So he had plenty to do on his end than to sit down and play $200/$400 with us. It wasn't unusual during the game for guys to be dropping off brown bags full of cash or him telling me stories about football games costing him $100k or more. I didn't bet sports just yet, but I was definitely curious about that whole other world.

This poker game was filled with the same concept of players but just stocked with more cash. Lots of the players were from the Board of Trade, lawyers, judges and just businessmen. We played 7 handed at the most because of the different variations of mix games we took on. I always had a baggie full of cash, usually $60k at most. I bought into the game for $20k and wanted to be able to have two more bullets in case I was running awful. The cash lied directly below me in my bag if I needed it to reload with. Other guys would walk in with backpacks or buy in with poker chips from the local casinos. They would smoke cigars and drink gin on the rocks and talk about the stock market all the time. They would always ask me how my week was since the game only got together on Thursday nights and they always seemed curious and inspired by what I was doing for a living. They were all great poker players surprisingly enough. But at the same time, all genius humans too, given their professions. We were all professionals at one point or another throughout the day and it was more of like a comfort feeling being accepted by them given my age and what I was doing with my life. As much as I wanted to fill them in and be social with them, I didn't really know what they were talking about half of the time. I was at the office. Right here and right now with them. This was my profession. Most of those guys all made over $1 million a year and some drover Ferrari's and Bentleys. I was still studying the game and wasn't even 21 yet. Even though it was the same game I was playing the day before at the Grand & Damen game and the previous few years, it was 5x the limit and much more intense. A couple of bad sessions here and I could lose 25% of my bankroll. I had to play smart and keep in mind the degree of the stakes I was playing.

The week after the fourth of July in 2006, I would have a night at the Skyscraper game that was unforgettable and my biggest win by far up to that point in my career. It's special to me even to this day. Because for poker players, a lot of guys can't recall huge pots they have won or the nights they won a ridiculous amount of money. Most poker players are so hard on themselves that they tend to only recall the fallouts and negatives of their careers. But tonight was special.

I arrived right around 6pm and there were two other players there already. Tyler had a chef on game nights along with the waitresses and he was cooking us ribs and steaks of all kinds. I didn't eat all day either. I had a late session the night before at the Grand & Damen game and lost about $2,300. I went home to sleep and woke up and came back to the city without skipping a beat. So I could eat anything at this point. I was ready to bounce back after a loss like that. Not only did it break my six winning sessions in a row, I was feeling down about a girl at that point in time and didn't want my poker game to be sidetracked because of her. Yes, even though I was living some fairy tale life I still had feelings and was still crazy for my high school sweetheart.

A couple of more players showed up and we decided to play $300/$600 instead. It seemed like the right crowd and if some of the regulars showed up, we could bring it back down to $200/$400 and add some games in too. Only exception, we were going to play straight hold em. Which was of course fine with me, I preferred the game straight. It went by faster than the mix games and was more profitable without the split pot games involved. We started out playing five handed $300/$600. I had about $80k on me so I was ok for now. I bought in for $20k and the night began.

The first hand I played was a pretty standard limit hand to say the least. I was in the big blind with Ad2d, we were still five handed and the button raised to $600, small blind folded and I called. The flop came up 3d6d2h, so I flopped bottom pair and the nut flush draw. A huge hand five handed. I decided to lead out and bet $300. He raised and I three bet to $900 and he called. The turn was another three and I led out for $600. He raised me to $1,200 and I called. River was another three, giving me the smallest full house possible. I checked and he bet of course. He could have easily had any pocket pair which I would obviously lose to. The only hand I could really beat was a missed flush draw such as mine. There was already almost $5k in the pot, so I figured I would call. I threw in six black chips like I wasn't interested at all and he said nice hand. He flipped over the Qd8d for a missed flush draw, pretty much the only type of hand that I could beat. I scooped that one and moved onto the next. The first hour I was up about $10k. Two other guys showed up and thankfully they decided to keep the stakes we were playing and to keep it as just hold em and we had an impressive lineup if I may say the least. Most of the regulars were in attendance and the game was equipped with lots of action and moving rapidly.

The next hand was ugly for my opponents, but quite the action. I had KhQh and two bet to $600. Two other guys called and the flop came out JdTh2c, flopping an open ended straight draw. I led out for $300 and got called on both parts. The turn was the 4h, giving me the straight flush draw now too. I led out for $600, got called and the guy on the button made it $1200 to go. I three bet to $1800 since I was already up about $20k and got called by both players. The river was an offset As giving me broadway (Ace high straight). I led out for $600 and got called on both spots. One guy had JT for two pair and the other guy on the button actually had a better flush draw than me with the Ah2h for a rivered two pair. I scooped the $9k pot and tipped the dealer $25.

The rest of the night would continue like this. It never ended really. Everything pretty much went right and before I knew it Tyler was busting out the $1k chips to color up the stack I had in front of me. It was one of the best runs I ever went on in Chicago. The sun was coming up and we were three handed and the limits had been $400/$800 for about the last three hours. The one guy was down to $1900 or so and we got it in on a Kxxxx board and I had K8. He mucked his hand and headed to the exit. The other guy that was left decided to call it quits too and I broke the game. I asked if he wanted to play heads up since he still had about $40k in front of him. We were pretty much the only two guys winning that night. He knew that heads up was one of my specialties, so he declined my challenge. I had $112k in front of me and was up $92k for the night. A run that to this day is remarkable to me.

The city games were a place of creation for me. A birth into what the high stakes world of poker was all about. The highs were the highs and the lows were the lows. It definitely let me get my feet wet before Vegas which was quickly approaching around the corner. The city games were a place where I experienced plenty of situations and accomplishments throughout my career that I needed in order to be successful in Vegas. I would continue to go to these games over the years. Not as often since I was about to turn 21 soon and would spend most of my time playing in Vegas and L.A. But once upon a time I heard that it's healthy to always return to your roots. They are the reason why you are where you are today. I have plenty of more memories than the ones listed above. Within all of these chapters it also develops other stories that could go on and on for a hundred pages probably. I put myself in dangerous situations all the time. Sometimes carrying around tens of hundreds of thousands of dollars in just brown lunch bags or backpacks, thinking it was my only option. In the end I survived. I lived through it all and I trained myself and got myself ready for Vegas. I think if I would have played those types of limits in Vegas for the first time that I would've lost and been too overwhelmed. Because it's Vegas and everything in that fucking town is magnified by a hundred to the third degree. Everything is harder there and every player is better than anywhere else.

Those were just two hot spots I used to go to. If I went on and on about the Chinatown game, Comiskey Park game, Bishop game, North End game, Lakefront game, Greek town game or the Church game, I would have a chapter that would just go on endlessly. All of those different games have their own life behind their titles. And each game served a different purpose in my growth in my career.

I was working too much and I needed a release. I was close to turning 21 and needed to party or something. I had been gambling every day since I left college. My two best friends from high school went to U of I and had been begging me to come down to visit. It was time that I head down to Champaign/Urbana to enjoy life on a different level.

"A drink does not exist. But whatever bullshit that comes out of a drunk's mouth that isn't logical, it is just the drink talking."

Champaign/Urbana-

I never really had a college experience at Lewis University. That freshman year that I was there was filled with 4am baseball practices, lots of sleeping and traveling. Whether I was traveling to a house game for poker or on the road with my team all over the Midwest, I didn't really spend a lot of time on campus. For baseball, we had curfews in the spring and workouts and practices in the afternoon in the fall. I didn't exactly have the same college experience as anyone that was in a frat house or at a large university. That really frustrated me and was something I was concerned about when I decided to leave school. That I would never know what that whole life experience felt like and I would miss out on those conversations down the road in life with my kids or old friends.

Lewis only had about 7,000 kids I think, which only maybe 2,000 lived on campus, if that. I think that it is very important for a college student to experience the full aspects of what college is all about. If you can walk out with a degree when it is all said and done, hats off and hold your head high to such an astonishing accomplishment. There are just as many bad influences in college as there are in anything else in the world. If not more because your maturity is still growing and experiencing new things. It's a warzone one day and a vacation the next. Coping with all of that is a tremendous learning experience.

My two best friends from high school went to the University of Illinois and had an apartment together. We texted and talked to each other on the phone all the time and mixed in with the establishment of social networking, we kept each other updated on our lives plenty so. They had been asking for me to come down for quite some time now. My days were consisted with constant gambling and they finally convinced me to make the ride down. I really needed it. I don't know if I was stressed out or just simply circling my life around constantly grinding and long extended nights that seemed to last forever. The sun became the moon and the moon became the sun. I definitely needed a change of scenery, even if it was just for a couple of days at a time. It would be healthy if anything. One problem, they were both heavy drinkers and I don't think I had ever been drunk in my life.

Ryan was my closest friend of all. We had been close since freshman year in high school and I had spent a lot of time at his house over the years and got very close with his parents and his twin sister. She was what I consider my high school sweet heart that I have already mentioned a couple of times. I know I know, sounds like an awful scenario. But through the handful of conversations him and I had about her over the years, he influenced and supported that decision and the thoughts we discussed. He always stated that he would rather have his best friend be with her that he trusted and knew cared for her, than some random guy he knew nothing about. It was also a sense of security I guess. I loved him for that decision. It truly meant a lot to me and just the trust he had expressed in our friendship as well.

Jeremy was a drama case, but we loved the kid. He and I had some issues during the first couple of years in high school, but we got really close towards the end of it before we graduated. We played baseball together and I seemed to be his big brother sort of. He was a mature kid but then again he wasn't. He called me in the middle of the night plenty of times crying about his ex-girlfriend looking for advice. Thinking that I had all the answers in life because of what I was doing with mine. But I didn't. He was a lightweight, but could drink all night. Quite the equation if you ask me. Ryan wasn't on the other hand. By no means was he an alcoholic either, but the kid could definitely hold his liquor. Ryan puked here and there, but I don't recall Jeremy ever getting sick.

I think it was the first week back to school in August when I came down. Which was pretty much considered a weekend full of drinking and partying in celebration of being back on campus. Seemed like the perfect time to make the 130 mile journey south down I-57 to get away from the city and make some bad decisions. It was like I was going to the Grand & Damen game for the first time all over again. I didn't know what to expect, I wanted to pick up some girls and talk to them and see where it led me. I had a ton of cash and all the confidence in the world in who I was and what I did for a living. Plus, I was turning 21 soon and had a future ahead of me. If anything, this was like a vacation and celebration. To be with your two best friends and having the time of your life, I don't think it gets much better than that at that age.

I packed a bag and headed south. I took the long way the first time down I-55 instead of I-57. I don't know why either. I arrived and parked across the street from their apartment. Was the first time I had ever been in a college town with the mindset that I had. Hot girls everywhere, frats that needed to clean up their garbage and people everywhere. Their apartment was just a two bedroom with one bathroom and a common area. It worked. It was also the first time that I was going to be meeting some of their college friends. Apparently Ryan and Jeremy had already premeditated who I was and what I did for a living to these guys and they welcomed me with open arms. They were full of questions and curiosity about some of my stories. Now, keep in mind that these guys were in frats and already had two years of being in college under their belts, I didn't. That's on all levels such as drinking, women and tolerance.

I walked in and they literally were already drunk and had a drink waiting for me. I introduced myself to his college buddies and we started up the classic pregaming that all college students came to know of. We were drinking captain and cokes and it was about 9pm I want to say. No one in college went out until 11pm, so we had time to get to know each other. Ryan was always the DJ of the crew. Always downloading new music and had the newest playlists ready and available for us to party to. We listened to pretty much any type of music, but we always fell back on rap and music from the 90's.

This was really the first time that I was going into a night intending on getting drunk. I had ordered us a couple of pizzas since some of the guys were hungry. I had about $2k on me, so I was hoping that would be enough cash for a weekend stay in a college town! I liked the taste of captain and coke. I wasn't used to it at all and I was highly tipsy after my first drink. By the time I was finished with my second I was telling everyone stories and my arms were around the guys I had just met. I was happy. I was with my new crew and all of them were awesome gents and they accepted me in right away. We went out and had a great time that night. We got food sometime around 1am completely wasted. My bed of choice was of course going to be one of the two couches in the front room whenever we made it back to the apartment. The three of us got back and I immediately went to the balcony they had and started puking three stories down into the alley. It was an awful feeling. But I was definitely helpless at this point. You just feel the eyes go in the back of your head and your eyes are filled with tears from the pressure and exhaustion. I didn't plan on puking 30 feet to the Earth's surface I swear, all I wanted was some fresh air. I promise you that I never did that again going forward, puked off the balcony that is. I finally finished up and headed back inside. I lied down and got my first experience of the spins. Any asshole that has never had the privilege of experiencing the spins can just walk to the exit. It is absolutely the most awful feeling. I didn't know this shit existed so I was freaking out when I was trying to fall asleep. It doesn't matter if your eyes are open or closed, but the room is spinning out of control. Someway somehow I got through it, but it would take me a long time until I didn't feel it anymore in the days to come.

Waking up in the mornings on their couch was always the worst. I was experiencing hangovers for the first time and they never had any food in the house or anything to drink to get through this dreadful feeling. By the time I woke up, they were either at class already or still passed out. I usually ordered a sub sandwich and they delivered it in under thirty minutes, so it was convenient for me. They didn't have any air conditioning if I remember right and given the fact that it was nearing the end of August, it was extremely hot outside. My best friend had some piece of shit fan blowing on me all night, but the sun was always blasting on me by the time I woke up. So it made any hangover that much more atrocious.

I spoiled these guys, but I wanted to. They were my best friends in the entire world and welcomed me in like we were in high school again. They told me I could stay for as long as I wanted to and I could come back whenever I wanted to as well. We would go out to dinners before we went out every night. We would all order delicious pastas or on other nights we would order the biggest steaks the restaurants had to offer. We would drink in style and in the end we just enjoyed being brothers and being together. I never had a problem picking up every tab because they were giving me an opportunity to live life away from the gambling scene. We would stop at the liquor store on the way back from dinner every time and I usually gave them a $100 budget and told them to get whatever they wanted. We would come back and pregame and go out and have the time of our lives. I would spend $300 on dollar drink night or give them money to buy drinks for other girls. I would buy entire trays of shots and pass them out to anyone that was around us. We always became pretty noticeable wherever we went. Plus, it helped that Ryan and Jeremy were popular guys too. We always had the best time anyone could possibly ask for.

But for the days I was down there, sometimes extended into 5-7 days at a time until I would come back to Chicago. I needed to find a way to work somehow in the meantime. PartyPoker of course was the answer to that. I had plenty of downtime during the day. They were both in class and sometimes I would wake up early and find food or wake up late and have nothing to do. So, Ryan was nice enough to let me download the software onto his computer which enabled me to grind for a few hours a day. I primarily played just $50/$100 and $100/$200. The $30/$60 games at this point usually had long lists and I never intended on playing more than a couple of hours at the most. So the higher stakes seemed like the way to go. This definitely made me feel better, because I had the opportunity to get some sessions in while they were at class and I didn't let a week slip by me. I was spending a lot of money while I was down there too. So this was a good way to make all of that back and then some. It also gave me the ability to keep me on my game and test myself as well. Playing online cash games, especially limit, took a special kind of talent. You were playing for thousands of dollars and the game moved incredibly fast. Every decision you made was important and magnified because you were going to be dealt about 120 hands an hour, compared to maybe 30 an hour in a live game. Those mistakes you might make throughout that extra time could really add up to a lot of cash by the end of a session.

I don't know how it started. Maybe it was going out every single night. But even on the nights that they didn't want to go out, I found myself in their kitchen making myself a drink. Or when they were away at class and I wanted to get a session in really quick, I couldn't play unless I was drinking. I liked the feeling I got of being numb and just experiencing a different side of life. I felt like I belonged by drinking and that I wasn't some outsider. I did what made me happy and drinking it was. My tolerance was getting a little bit better, but I still experienced the spins and still puked at the end of the night. But, I was definitely getting better. Not that that is anything to brag about either.

Ally was Ryan's twin sister that I briefly mentioned before. I had been going on about six years of having a crush on her. We actually briefly dated in high school and we were extremely close as well. Ryan and I spent a lot of time together in high school, so I was always running into her if I came over to their house to hang out with Ryan. She also went to U of I and only lived a few blocks away from Ryan's apartment. I would be lying if I said that some of the reason I came down to see Ryan and Jeremy wasn't to see Ally. But she was a book nerd and all of us knew that, even her. We would always try and get her to come out with us. Or I would always try and get her to meet me for lunch or just anything really. We had a couple of nights where I had to walk her home from being too drunk and I would spend the night. We never had sex, although we could have. I just didn't feel like it was right. Regardless of what I had going on in my life and the guy I had become, I respected this girl. She and her family meant a lot to me and if we were ever going to engage in finally having sex, I wanted it to be for the right reasons. She knew this. I think one of the best nights her and I ever had, I walked her home from 5th street because she was absolutely hammered. We got back to her place and we fell asleep on the couch together. In the morning I woke up alone and she was in bed. She eventually woke up and I took a shower. She made us lunch and when we were finished, we washed the dishes together, and then I kissed her gently on the cheek and held her from behind. It was just an enjoyable moment with someone that meant the world to me. Those moments to this day I obviously haven't forgotten about and I will always hold deep to my heart.

U of I was important to me from the summer of 2006 until the spring of 2008. I would go from

Chicago to there and back and when I started going to Vegas all the time, I would go from Vegas to Midway airport, drive to Champaign and then back to the airport again. If I had a guess as to how many times I made my way down to Champaign in that 20 months or so, my guess would have to be near 50. I had a chance to live my college experience down there since I missed out on my chances at Lewis. I was able to throw on a backpack and blend in with the rest of the kids like I went to school there. It kind of felt like a different type of acceptance to be honest, to become a normal 20 something year old again. It was kind of like my sense of reality. The guys knew what I did of course, but it was very gratifying to just let life come back to earth again when I was down there.

I've had plenty of debates with myself, but I am pretty sure that my alcohol problem stemmed from that town, on all counts. It wasn't from Vegas or private luxurious games in Chicago. It came from a college town. Just as expected. I wonder sometimes to this day how many kids left that town, whether with a degree or not with an alcohol problem. Maybe I was so caught up in the life I was living 2,000 miles away or the other one in Chicago's underground life that I was vulnerable to what a regular 20 year old kid should be doing with his life. I wanted to experience all of those things more intensely to make sure I was going to be able to talk about them sometime down the road in my life. Once I was able to tolerate the booze, given the no responsibility life I had and endless amounts of cash flow, I couldn't really control myself anymore. I was drunk every day I was in Champaign and just about every day going forward too.

Just like the rest of the experiences I had early on in my career, I don't regret any of them. I am glad that I had my own little entourage of friends down at U of I. It was probably the only balance I had back then. The two hour drive from the airport was more therapeutic than any plane ride or sunset. It was my place of peace where I could get away from the money or interviews and intense lifestyle I had developed in Vegas, L.A. and Chicago. I miss it. And I miss those guys. I wish that I had more maturity back then that I could have treasured those moments more than I thought they were actually worth. I didn't and I have learned to deal with those feelings a little bit better every day. Every trip was worth it and a little bit more every time I hopped back on the highway to go back to Vegas, I felt like I was going back with a purpose. That it was to make my friends proud and appreciative of the gambler that I had become.

But, it was time. I was ready. I had spent every day for the last four years waiting for the day that I could finally go to Vegas.

Happy 21st birthday, Nicholas.

"Anything that happened in Vegas, didn't stay in Vegas."

1,730 Miles & a Carry On-

I turned 21 years old, finally. Everyone I knew was asking me when I was going to adventure out to Vegas once and for all. They figured I would have been there by now. I had some things I needed to take care of back in Chicago before I headed out there. I wasn't too sure how long I was going to stay to be honest. That first trip could last either a few hours or a few weeks. I wanted to make sure that before I left, I had the capability of being away for a while. For the first time in my career I kind of sat down and had a lot of conversations with myself

and what I was planning on doing while I was there. I had already developed the experience of being inside casinos and everything from going to Canterbury, but I mean this was Vegas. Everything was going to be more intense, even the food. Vegas had a million more poisonous ingredients and temptations than that of the situations I had previously put myself into. All of the elements I have been in were all controlled settings. The private games in the city to the regular casino in Minnesota. Now you throw Vegas in the mix, it's a warzone to a professional poker player. From everyone being high or intoxicated to the hookers and I didn't even get to the gambling portion of it yet. I don't think I need to throw all of them down on paper for you to understand what I am talking about.

My parents knew that it was only a matter of time until I told them I was hopping on a plane to go to Vegas on a regular basis. My mother was supportive and still is supportive of anything I have done in my life as long as I was safe and it was for a good purpose. My father on the other hand is just a natural born cynic, but he means it in a good way. So that I can take what he is saying from someone else's point of view and apply it to my life in that . stature on my own and in my own way and on my own path. He can take any conversation and turn it into a meaningful life purpose topic. It's just how he is. Over the course of the next three years of my traveling back and forth, I am sure we touched on every life topic imaginable.

My mom cried when I told her for the first time that the time had come for me to travel west. She was used to me being gone and the traveling that I did to

Canterbury, but this was obviously just a little bit more extreme on all counts. I think my father just told me to be safe and let him know I was ok and to check in when I could. I don't think I could have had the success I did if I didn't prep myself at Canterbury for a year straight. That's one respect I always gave to both of my parents. Here's their only child putting himself in situations and staying away from home for days on end and in dangerous scenarios, the least I could do was to check in with them a couple of times a day. Just to let their mind slow down and know that I am alright. I definitely conserved that promise to them. A simple text or phone call was all that was needed.

It was a week after my birthday and I was lying in bed watching television. I had a brutal session the night before at the Skyscraper game and dropped about $24k playing $200/$400 mix. Yes, even I had losing sessions. They weren't too often, but they did happen. I had just gotten home actually around noon. I slept at the apartment where the game was at because I am sure I had about fifteen captain and cokes that night. Tyler and I had become pretty close since I was a regular in his game, and he always wanted me to crash at his place if I had too much to drink. Worst part about waking up is that drive all the way back home to the distant suburbs. I lived an hour away from the city and I always tried to get out of there before rush hour hit, or else the duration of the enduring ride practically doubled. I was still pretty hung over, but I had grown such a competitive attitude that when I had losing sessions, I had to play the next day. I wasn't the kind of player that just let losing sessions dwell on me and for the progression in my career I was moving towards, I had to always play the following day to regroup. That obsession to play the following day after a loss of any kind was just my devotion and love for the game. Not the growing demon inside of me that was getting larger by the day at its own speedy pace.

I had gotten a call from a buddy of mine that he had some money he owed me from a few weeks prior. Unfortunately, if I wanted it I had to drive to the casino to pick it up. He had a winning session the night before in a $10/$25 NL game that was ran on Friday nights at the local casino just outside of Chicago in Gary, IN. A lot of players back then would just live at that casino. The rooms were gorgeous and big enough to sleep four guests comfortably. The players had so many comps that you could literally just make a couple of phone calls and you had a free room for a week if you wanted to just live at the boat and grind cash games. I told him I would be there in a couple of hours and I packed a bag thinking I would just stay there for the weekend. Saturday nights they ran some nice limit games and the high rollers would come in from the city. The limits never got higher than $50/$100 really, but the games were huge with action. I grabbed $20k from my safe and headed to Indiana.

I got there rather quickly and grabbed a drink at the steak house bar in the lobby. I had become a fan of long islands as of recently, I ordered a tall one and threw the bartender a $20 bill and told him to keep the change. Since I had been a poker dealer and still was some nights and working off of tips only, I knew how important each tip meant. It was a gratifying feeling going forward to over tip or catch waitresses or bartenders off guard with large sums of tips. Felt good to give back to strangers.

I grabbed my bag and headed up to Larry's room. He really was a good guy. He was in his 30's an alcoholic, degenerate sports betting junkie, but a very skilled poker player. Recently divorced because of his gambling habits, but thankfully enough he didn't have any children. He was just one of those guys where one day he was broke and the next day he had $10k somehow. But, when that moment arrived, he had to pay back whoever he had borrowed the money from originally. Because word of mouth travels extremely fast in the poker world, especially if people know that you owe others money, they won't hesitate to make a phone call on your behalf to let that other party aware of your recent winnings. I was proud of him that he contacted me right away on his big score. Just in general I think that at one point I had 30 guys that owed me over $100k total. I knew that some of it I would never see again, but most of them were pretty good at paying me back or making payments. I never hounded any of them for it and I didn't charge any interest. They trusted me and I trusted them too. It was just something that you did in the poker world. Sometimes you were playing against each other at the tables, but other times it was comforting to know that you had an army of guys behind you that would help you out if need be. I would regret that openness later on in my career that you will find out about in the chapters to come, but as for Larry, I was excited to hear about the details from the night before.

I knocked on his door and he let me in with a smile on his face. My bag was heavier than usual since I assumed I was staying for at least five days and I threw it down on the floor by the desk. One of our buddies Zach was passed out in one of the beds and there was some cocaine on the nightstand and a pile of cash next to it. He gave me a hug and handed me seven bright orange $1k chips. He owed me $10k, but asked if we could keep the other $3k on the books for now. I said of course and stashed the chips down in my pocket. He told me all about the night before and a blackjack session he had afterwards, by the end of the night he was up about $30k. I was happy for him. He was one of the good guys back then. Always in a good mood and just looking to finally hit a big score. He said he won about $17k in the cash game and another $13k playing blackjack. He owed $15k so he had a little bankroll of about $14-$15k now.

We grabbed a quick bite to eat and another round of drinks and it was about 6pm. We went upstairs to the poker room and it was absolutely packed. Just because I was who I was didn't mean that I could just skip ahead on lists either. I had to wait just like everyone else. There weren't any empty tables either in case we wanted to start up something new. There were five high stakes games going with a long list of people waiting for them. Larry suggested we throw our names on the list and go downstairs and play blackjack. I agreed and we made our way back down the escalator.

I wasn't a big blackjack fan. I never got into it even though it was available for me in Minnesota. I really just stuck to poker up to this point in my career since it's what I was good at. I had no reason to change anything up since I was doing just fine with it. All of the regular tables downstairs in the pits were extremely crowded as well being Saturday night and all. We made our way to the high limit room and sat down at an empty $100 minimum table. I pulled out a couple of the $1k chips he paid me back with upstairs and we began. I had the dealer change them up for a rack of blacks, which are $100 each. We ordered another round of drinks and the first $2k for me disappeared in about eight minutes. Like I mentioned, Larry was a junky. He was up about $2500 in the same amount of time. I told him to just throw me the $2500 he just won and we can call it even on the $3k he owed me. He couldn't say no and we were even, which is always a good feeling. Things started to heat up and I forgot about the $20k I also brought with me. So just for shits sake, I started to bet higher. Not that I probably couldn't go upstairs to the poker room and gather up $5k or so in debt owed to me. But regardless of the fact, I started to bet $500 a hand minimum. Maybe it was the booze, but I was just in a good moment with a close friend of mine and felt the increase in stakes applied. We were drunk, he was up about $5k and I won my first four hands with a double down so I had won back about $2,500. If you want to count in the $2k I lost, I was only up $500.

We continued to play for another hour or so and decided to call it quits. He was up $6,400 and I was up $3,700. Out of respect he threw me a purple chip, which was the remaining $500 I let him slide on. This was my point, little moments like that. Where respect was shown and given and received. Poker players had more respect for each other than anyone I have met to this day. It is just a certain bond you gather when you're out there grinding cash games or tournaments together. Spending more time next to each other than you spend with your families, you become brothers. You will never truly understand that respect until you live through what a poker player has to go through and deal with each and every day.

We started to head back to the poker room to check on the waiting list and Larry kind of stopped me at a breaking point where I could either turn right and head towards the exit and the hotel, or go left and head up the escalator to go back to the poker room.

"What are you still doing here anyway?"

I asked him what he meant and he looked me right in the face and laughed.

"You're the best player I know and you just turned 21. Why weren't you on a plane to Vegas eight days ago? Do us both a favor, head back to my room and get your stuff, go to the airport and catch the late flight to Vegas. Indiana is the last place you should be. You deserve it to yourself if anything to head out there."

I gave him a hug and made my way towards the exit and back up to the room to get my bag. I didn't have to make a stop back home for more cash. I brought $20k, just won about $4k and Larry paid me back the $10k he owed me. So the $35k in my pocket was more than enough to go to Vegas with.

I started making my way towards the airport. It was pretty cold being the end of November, so I was looking forward to feeling a little bit of desert heat on my skin. Or the most it could offer me this time of year. Fuck, the feelings that were coming over me as I made my way into the parking garage were almost making me tear up. I was finally going to Vegas! I wondered how much a one way flight would be and if I was too late. I kept asking myself what hotel I would stay at. It was Saturday night, I am sure the strip was crowded with tourists. What game was I going to play? I had to go to Bellagio first and damn I couldn't wait to see the lights on the strip. I have seen them a million times on the television these last few years, but it was all finally going to become a reality. It was almost 7:30 at night and I was afraid the last flight was going to be impossible to catch. I kind of ran into the check in area and started praying.

"Hi, hoping there's a late flight to Vegas?"

"Sure is, but you're going to have to run to catch it. It departs at 8:10."

I asked for a one way ticket and handed over $185. Not too bad I guess. A major increase to the $65-$80 I was spending on one way flights to Minneapolis. She handed me my ticket and I walked as fast as I could in the direction of the terminal. I had about thirty minutes to get to the gate and the airport was surprisingly empty. Nothing is more exhausting than getting to security check and the line is a mile long. But! In the future I never had to face that problem anyways. Since I always bought my ticket the day of the flight and with cash, I had to go through a separate security line that was off to the side and that never had anyone in it. That was always convenient and a time saver to not have to wait in line with the rest of the world before every flight.

I made it. Of course it was the last gate all the way at the end, but nonetheless they were almost finished with boarding. The one downfall about buying your ticket the day of traveling and on an open seating flight was that you were usually the last one to board the plane. Come to think of that, I only had to sit in a middle seat maybe a handful of times. Keep in mind that I wanted to fly in college and be a pilot someday. My eventual dream was to be up in the skies just flying above the world with the angels. I always tried my hardest to find a window seat to enjoy the view, didn't matter if it was night or day. I boarded and found a window seat towards the back on the right side of the plane if you're looking forward towards the cockpit. The flight was extremely empty, about half full, so I had my own row in the back. That was always peaceful in case you wanted to lie down and catch a nap.

So, they went through their normal speech of getting the flight ready to depart and we made our way to the runway. I couldn't help but stare out the window with a different attitude than as if I was flying to traditional Minneapolis again. I was headed to the center of the gambling world, the mecca for poker. With nothing but confidence under my belt and what I thought was enough experience up to this point in my young career, to compete with the best in the world. I knew that I was proud of myself at the moment, but I had no idea what I was about to encounter with in Vegas. Everything about that town is overwhelming if you aren't ready and fully prepared for it.

Lift off, wheels up.

We leveled out and the view outside of my window was just a dark blanket and the clouds were floating on by like they were ghosts of the sky. You put your nose up to the window to see the world below and the little towns light up their boundaries like it's all they own. Sometimes it was as if you weren't even moving. As if we were just hovering in the air and not going 600 miles per hour.

"Can I have a jack and coke please?"

I was wide awake and the next three and a half hours were going to feel like three and half days. That's the worst isn't it? When you're so excited to do something and time just seems to mock you and takes its own time, making you strain on your thoughts and twitch. I was about five drinks in when the captain came on the intercom and did his speech. He updated us and made us aware that we were 45 minutes outside of Vegas's city limits. I had a couple of tears fall down my face more than once in the last couple of hours. I wondered what everyone back home was doing, or what I was missing out on. I missed my friends at U of I a lot and Ally too. But I couldn't stop thinking about just finally being there. The challenges I was going to come in contact with and what players I would be playing against in just a couple of hours, or what stakes.

My sight never left looking out the window and the earth had been completely dark for a while now. Flying over the mountains and the desert, there's just nothing out there. Every once and a while you would see a random establishment or some type of business hardly lit up twenty thousand feet below. Then all of a sudden a strand of orange lights appeared. Just a small amount at first and they got bigger and bigger the closer we got to the airport.

"We will begin our final descent into Las Vegas. It'll be about 10:05 local time and it is 68 degrees. We thank you all for flying with us and welcome to Vegas."

We crossed over the mountains and there it was. Vegas. Palm trees everywhere, smaller casinos off the strip and a pool in every backyard. Then the strip appeared and it was just like it was on television. But fuck me it was overwhelming. The lights were brighter than expected and the hotels and casinos were the biggest buildings I had ever seen. It was like I was being dropped off in the middle of the jungle by a helicopter during the war with no directions. Good luck and survive pretty much. I'll be here when you get back from your mission. I had to treat every trip like it was a mission or else this town was going to suck me in entirely. Yes, I was coming out here for higher limits and more experience and to face the best of the best. But every negative ingredient to destroy a life can be found in this town. Whether you're prepared for those demons or not, you're going to face them every day.

I walked off the plane and through the path of humans to make it to the taxi line. The automatic doors opened up and the desert heat hit me in the face. The cab line was a ghost town and I threw my bag in the trunk of the next available cab.

"Welcome to Vegas, sir. Where to now?"

"Bellagio, please."

It just seemed like the most fitting place to start my first trip out on. All these years I had been playing in private games in the city with these millionaires, they always said I had to play at Bellagio first. That it had the most action and the highest stakes in the world. I figured I would pray they had an empty room for me on a Saturday night.

I arrived and I had never seen a hotel like this. Everything was marble and every girl was beautiful. All of the flowers were of colors I didn't even knew existed. The smell inside the lobby was the purest of pure. Everything about everything was just perfect. I couldn't stop looking around because it was like a city street walking through the Bellagio. People are everywhere, drunk, laughing, dressed to impress, smiling and gorgeous. From the famous to the poor, Bellagio was as luxurious as you got in that town and I hadn't even left the lobby yet.

I stood behind a European couple checking in. Anxiously waiting for them to leave so that I could find out if there were rooms available and I could sink it all in and get started.

"Welcome to Bellagio sir, how can I help you?"

"I am praying to God that you have rooms available on a Saturday night if possible and for a few days too?"

They did. I asked for three nights, figured that was a safe amount of time to start with. If I went broke with the $35k I had buried in my bag, I could at least walk around Vegas for the remaining time and get to learn the town. I obviously planned on spending a lot of time here in the years to come. I coughed up $685 for the three nights and she gave me my confirmation receipt and room keys.

"Sir, you're staying on the 9th floor. Here are directions to your room and your keys. Just turn around and head down this row right behind you until you hit the craps tables and turn left. The elevators will be on your right."

I started the walk and shit, was I like a little kid in a candy store again. There were table games everywhere and 90's music playing on the overhead speakers. Every table was crowded and action just painted the room from wall to wall. Women were beautiful, guys were good looking and everyone had on gold and diamonds. I hit the craps tables and turned left. Flashed my key to the security guard and made my way up to my room. The room was incredible. Just a regular room was even luxurious in so many different ways. There were twenty pillows on each bed and a view facing the strip and the famous fountain. Equipped with a huge flat screen, marble everything and a full bar. I set the room temperature to 67 degrees, unpacked a couple of things and looked in the mirror. I think I was finally ready to head downstairs and be a real professional poker player. I grabbed $30k from my bag and stashed it all into my pockets. Threw the other $5k in the room's safe and headed downstairs in search of the poker room.

I stopped at the lounge bar that overlooked the fountain and got a double jack and coke. My buzz from the plane had worn off by this point. It was about 11pm, which is early in Vegas for anything really. I wanted to just go outside and walk around the strip, but I had to see this poker room. I knew it was going to be overwhelming and astounding. Bellagio actually had a large tournament series going on, so all of the pros were in town for it. I hadn't even hit the poker room yet and I had already seen the likes of a few of the top 10 players in the world. Even to this day.

I heard the chips and could see the tables. I walked in and the room was just packed. To this day I have never seen so much action in my life. Thirty plus tables down below, five more up in the high stakes room and two more in Bobby's Room, would pretty much sum up the entire room. Bobby's Room was the Yankee Stadium of poker. It had two tables inside of it and that's where the elite of the elite played the highest stakes in the world. They played limits such as $1k/$2k NL and $4k/$8k mix on a daily basis. The room was filled with the best of the best. I tried not to be like a tourist and stare inside, but I just couldn't help myself for a few seconds. Across from me there were six tables of $100/$200 limit hold em and all of the limits below that can be offered. In the high stakes room a couple of steps up behind them were two tables of $200/$400 and two other tables of $25/$50 NL and a $300/$600 mix game. In the $300/$600 game the dealer had about ten plates next to him with the names of the games that they were playing. He would leave the plate of the game they were currently playing on top of the rest for convenience for the players to know which game they were on. The game was completely identical to the Skyscraper game back home in Chicago, fitting right? I asked the floor man if there was a seat available and he said yes. I handed him $20k to run and get me two racks of $100 chips from the cage. I sat down and it was time. Time for me to take everything I had taught myself and apply it. Only problem was, I was nervous as fuck. He brought my chips over to me and I was actually shaking as I dumped them out and lined them up in front of me. Did I mention that David Singer was on my right and Mark Gregorich was in the corner seat? Just a couple of the best limit players in the world that I have been watching on television these last couple of years.

"Do you want something to drink sir?"

My god was she the most beautiful woman I had ever seen in my life with a body to die for.

"A double jack and coke please".

The chips were perfect. You could stack them eighty high if you wanted to be obnoxious. The cards were perfect and the dealers never messed up a single pitch or hand if they wanted to it seemed like. The action was fast and the plays were impeccable. These players were phenomenal. Everything they did was practiced and in a routine over and over. How they bet and the styles in which they bet. How they tipped the dealers and the value bets they made. I was learning something new and being as observant as I possibly could be during each hand at the same time. I was right there with them and up about $8k in the first hour. We were actually only playing seven games. All variations of H.O.R.S.E. and also Badugi and 2-7 Triple Draw. Pretty much the sexiest line up of games ever created.

The drinks were flowing and before I knew it, it was about three in the morning and I was wasted.

We were five handed and I was up about $25k. I loved short-handed limit games. They were fast paced and on point. Decisions were made in seconds and not minutes. You developed patterns and discovered flaws. You changed up your game based off of the action and flow of the betting. Over time you just simply acquired your own rhythm that defined your game and who you were as a poker player. That's why it was easy for me to shrink down in limits a tenth of this size and be able to single out each player's psyches and know exactly what kind of a player they were in just a few encounters. How aggressive they were and if they had the capability of check raising me in certain spots. If they did, to think three steps ahead of them in a matter of seconds and check my option just to have them bet like idiots and I raise them back. But all of those thoughts became natural to me after a while.

I finished up my session and I won about $20k. What a shocking first experience that was. To sit down in a game of that magnitude and to be surrounded by that kind of talent, just to come out on top was a very gratifying feeling. For whatever reason with it being my first night in Vegas, I felt it appropriate to keep on drinking and walk around the strip some. I found myself another long island and at this point I was probably about seven or eight drinks deep. I ordered room service while I was at the table, so at least I had some food in my stomach. The strip was full and everyone was in groups and having a great time. It was the best place to people watch if you're a fan of that. I personally am very much. People are their own aliens really. It's quite interesting sometimes if you just watch the world go by.

I made my way back to Bellagio around six in the morning. Stumbling and exhausted. I held an empty drink in my hand, but still owned a large sum of curiousness that was floating around my imagination in regards to this town. I made my way past the closed restaurants and groups of leftover drunks trying to keep themselves on their own two feet. When I cashed out earlier, I cashed out in large chips, so I had $41k in my pocket. I remembered the short run of blackjack I had the day before with Larry, and decided to sit down at a vacant table just before the lobby and find a second wind to keep on gambling. I don't really know if this was the beginning to a self-destruct demoralization of my career that would take a couple more years to come to an end, but the more and more that I played blackjack, the more I was silently sabotaging my poker career and giving birth to a fearless degenerate demon inside of me.

I figured it was safe to just buy in with the $20k I just won a few hours prior playing poker. Playing with your profits was never realistic to me. Like some guys I knew, would win like $22,800 and then go play blackjack with $2,800 of it since $20k was an even number. They wouldn't have any problems losing that $2,800 either since it was like tacked on money to them. To me, money was money. I had such a strong competitive nature that I had compiled over the years from playing sports and then playing poker these last three years, that I just had to win every time I played. Trying to win every time you play blackjack is not realistic though. Sure I went on unbelievable winning streaks playing poker.

Streaks that to this day I have never heard anyone else go on. My best ever was I won 34 sessions in a row at Canterbury playing $30/$60. It was such a non-realistic number to be honest, given all of the variations and scenarios looking back on it. But, when you're in the zone, I guess you're just simply in the zone. I built up a tolerance for winning because of this. My cocky dumbass thought that I could mirror those results playing blackjack.

I bought in for $20k and threw the dealer one of the flags. Oh, by the way we called $5k chips "flags" because they were red, white and blue. By far one of the sexiest names and chips of all time if you had to ask me, maybe it's just because those were the largest denomination of chips I had ever held up to that point. And it stayed with me until now. But those chips were noticeable and respectable anywhere in Bellagio. They caught the attention of the floor men and tourists alike.

"Change please."

She changed me up with $4k in $500s and another $1k in $100s and I started my morning off with a $200 bet. The mornings there didn't exist, or more so, the concept of time in Vegas didn't exist. Sometimes I would figure out the time of day based off of people's outfits and the capacity of the casino. If girls were walking around in bathing suits and sunglasses, they were on their way to the pool, so it was safe to say that it was somewhere around noon. If they were sober and walking around in dresses, it was the beginning of the evening. And if they were stumbling around the casino and couldn't speak English anymore, it was somewhere around two in the morning. Sometimes I would play blackjack for 24 hours straight, sometimes longer. By that point in time I would be highly intoxicated and my blackberry would be dead. I had to find other means of time. Since I usually had on some $18k watch and a hat pulled down low, betting so high to the point where the floor man would change the title of the table to show reserved, I pretty much just tried to focus on the action in front of me. Leaving me an empty and lonely guy most of the time I was out there. Safe to say that I wasn't too much of a social guy back then unless I was back home in Chicago somewhere. I never turned down a conversation in Vegas really, but at the same time I never started one up either.

Sorry for that quick flashback there, but she gave me my change and I began. It was still my first night in Vegas and maybe that's why I caught my second wind at six in the morning. I had waited so long to be here, that I was still taking it in with every card that was being dealt and every bet that I was winning and even losing. I felt at peace and at home with what I was doing with my life. A feeling that I don't think I had ever discovered in any other establishment. Each element gives you different feelings and thoughts to move forward with. Maybe it took me finally coming here to experience that. But I had been there less than 12 hours and I was in for quite the treat.

The first $10k was gone before I even got my first drink, somewhere around 6:15 in the morning. She brought me a long island and a shot of tequila. Since I was betting upwards of $1,500 a hand, I asked the floor man if it was ok if I ordered breakfast from the room service menu and had it delivered right where I was. He laughed and obliged.

"Anything for you kid."

I had about $27k in front of me and was betting $500-$1,500 a hand. I had won back $17k from when I lost that first $10k in just a matter of a few minutes. That's one thing about blackjack and anyone that has played it will understand this, it's a game of runs. Sometimes you can win fifteen hands in a row and other times, none of it makes sense. I have been lined up with four hands of double downs against a dealer showing a six and been scooped for upwards of $50k. The list goes on. Sometimes it's just not your day.

My breakfast showed up finally and it was the funniest thing I had ever seen. To this day I have never seen room service catered to a blackjack table. Given the fact that it was seven in the morning and there were only three tables open, I guess it seemed acceptable. I looked down at scrambled eggs, bacon, toast and a delicious piece of steak, what more could a drunk ask for at this time of day? Total came out to $28 and I gave the lady a $100 bill and told her to keep the rest. The questions began to scramble, but I asked her to bring me another drink and we can call it even. She smiled and I went back to playing.

I wanted more money in front of me for whatever reason. I had pulled out the other $20k in flags that were in my pocket at some point, and before I knew it I had about $75k in front of me. Life was good. My bankroll was somewhere around $450k, I was in Vegas for the first time, intoxicated and had no responsibilities but to take care of myself. Anyone on the planet would agree with me right now when I say that I should have finished my breakfast, gone up to my room and call it a successful first night in Vegas and get some rest. I was up $42k between poker and blackjack. I was wide awake at this point, even though I was going on 24 hours of being up. I decided to slow it down a little bit on the drinking and just ordered a jack and coke and kept on playing.

Noon rolled around and things weren't going my way at all. I had dumped back about $55k and was left with $20k in front of me. I was taking an extremely brutal beating on several hands that in theory, the book says should go my way. I wasn't being dealt any blackjacks either. Just a lot of 13s-16s against face cards that I can't do much about except hit and pray. I bet $2k on a hand and got dealt two 8s against the dealer showing a 5. I split them and threw another $2k on the split 8, the dealer gave me a 2 and I opted to double down on it. She swiped off a 9 giving me a 19, which isn't horrible. On the other 8 she gave me a 3 and I decided to double down on that one too. Only leaving me $1k in front of me if I somehow lose this hand, but I wasn't panicking. It was a good spot for me to win some money back. She gave me an 8 on the double down giving me 19. So I had two 19s in front of me for $8k out there, $16k if I win both. She flipped over a king and then another 5 giving her 20 and scooping me. I threw the floor man the remaining $1k chip in front of me and told him to split that amongst the dealers. Grabbed my drink and started to make the walk of shame back to my room.

I had never lost that much money before. I forgot that I still had $5k upstairs in my room in my safe. So in theory on the day I lost $30k. But, I was up about $45k-$50k at one point. That was the exhausting number that was bothering me. Don't forget, two days before that I lost $24k at the Skyscraper game too. Two days, $100k. I went from the king of the world a few hours before to the loneliest guy in Vegas. I needed to take this in as an experience and somehow learn from it, even though it was an expensive one. At the same time, if I was going to make gambling an occupation of mine, I needed to also learn how to lose. I needed to take some knowledge from the emotion I was feeling and learn to get past it and deal with it. Or I was never going to be successful in this town or in this life either.

I got back to my room and my fucking key card didn't work for some reason and I had to go all the way back downstairs to the front desk to get a new one. That walk of course felt like it was a lifetime away. I made my way back downstairs, past the table I had just sat at for eight hours and lost all of that cash and up to the front desk. I told her my situation and she verified my identity and gave me a new card. I made my way back down the walk of shame, which I have already taken previously a few times now and back up to my room.

Only thing I realized this time though, my room number that was on my new key certification, was on the left side of the hallway instead of on the right where it wasn't working. Confused as fuck, I tried it anyways, door opened and there was all of my shit. So when my key couldn't work twenty minutes earlier, it's because I was trying it on the room directly across the hallway from me. Shit. It was around two in the afternoon and I had two options. Either I got some rest and slept as much as I could, woke up and gambled with my remaining $5k I had in my safe, or I grabbed my shit and headed to the airport immediately. Giving Vegas a much needed goodbye salute, go home, get $100k and come back and destroy this town. So, I did just that.

Regardless of the fact that I had been up longer than 30 hours given the two hour time change, I figured that I could sleep on the plane, get home, rest some more, grab some cash and head on back to Vegas. Hopefully just play poker this time around. I would still be sleeping right now with $60k in my safe had I gone that route the night before. But, we all make fucking mistakes. Before I even had the opportunity to unpack my bag or enjoy my amazing bed and sheets, I grabbed everything and headed to the airport. That was one of the best things about flying out of Vegas, there was a flight available pretty much every hour for any airline whether you were coming or going. Given that, it always made for an easy escape from that town a possibility if you wanted to get the hell outta dodge.

I woke up to the feel of the wheels scraping against the Chicago runway. I had slept the entire flight home and I barely even remember taxiing out of Vegas. Safe to say I needed the rest. If you have been trying to figure it out, my first trip came and went and I spent about 18 hours in Vegas. Did you really expect anything more? I did the big old stretch and was actually happy to be home even though I was gone for only a day. I don't even really know if I experienced any type of a full affect as to what Vegas was all about. I was drunk the whole time, had one of the biggest swings of my career and didn't really have a plan when I landed. The short trip was completely spontaneous.

I finally found my car and made my way back to my house. It was late, almost midnight by the time I got back on the road. I figured that I would head home, sleep as much as possible and when I eventually decided to wake up and get out of bed I would head back to Vegas. I didn't have to pack another bag or anything since I never even broke open the zipper on this one. I got home around one in the morning and crashed. What an interesting almost 24 hours.

I woke up somewhere in between the morning and the afternoon. I forgot the day and my mother was on the phone talking to someone. Yes, I had half a million dollars almost and still lived at home. I didn't really see the need of getting my own place just yet since I had planned on spending a lot of time out on the west coast or just in general on the road.

"Home already?"

She silently hated everything that I was doing. Part of her trusted me and still supported this out of left field headed for a disaster kind of lifestyle. All of those demoralizations were all still so blind to me. I didn't know what losing was yet. I knew that I had a future in what I was doing. It was important to me in a thousand ways really. I wanted to be a daddy someday. It is my ultimate goal in life even to this day to be a father, settle down and have a family. If anything, it was my only motivation back then. A little human that I had never even met yet, was already the world to me.

"Yep, I'm headed back tonight, though."

I took a shower, got dressed and picked up my bag off the floor that still hadn't been opened yet in almost 48 hours. Grabbed $100k out of my safe and headed out the door. I never left my house without giving my mother a huge hug and kiss. She deserved it. She was a perfect mother and always will be to me. She deserved every good bye and every good morning I gave her.

I was pissed and extremely upset with myself to be honest. All I ever thought about was my play the day after. And maybe it took some sobering up and a good night sleep for it to kick in to realize what I did the day before in Vegas. It wasn't who I was. I truly hoped that it was just a first time in Vegas kind of moment that I had, or at least the alcohol. I kept looking for some type of excuse without admitting to myself that I was acquiring a hidden addiction that was if anything, more dangerous than anything else in that town. I will let you decide whether I am talking about blackjack or the booze.

So, I made the ride again. Back to the airport and back to a place that would honestly become a second home to me over the years. Not just Vegas, but the airports as well. The employees began to know me as did a couple of the vendors. I had plenty of time to people watch. I had plenty of time to sit there in those little uncomfortable seats that surround the terminal gates and just watch the world. Just watch it as it went by. Somehow the piano music in the distance of my mind would always catch me off guard in those moments. I would try all the time to find little moments in life that were special to me. Since a lot of my time consisted of me sitting around a poker table with no balance, I made sure that whenever I had the opportunity to take in the little moments that life showed itself, I tried my best to capture them. Down the road, I came back to blaming a lot of that on maturity. The more things that I experienced, the more life opened itself up to me. I appreciated things more as another day came and went.

I woke up about an hour into the flight I want to say. I ordered a jack and coke and went back to staring out the window like usual. The sun was just setting and I was just kind of enjoying it. Plane rides gave you that few hours to just stare out the window and think about life. I had all of these different lives too. I had my home life with my family, I had my city game life, Vegas life and my U of I life. I missed my friends a lot. I would probably drive back to Champaign after this trip to just get back to some stage of reality for a few days. Even though it would consist of more drinking and partying, essentially it's what I should be doing when I was 21 years old anyway. Not living in and out of airports and losing tens of thousands of dollars every day.

About five more drinks would come and go off my tray before we started to make our final descent into Vegas. I had a feeling of déjà vu come over me since I was just in this exact seat and enjoying this exact view just a day before. We landed and there was the strip. I had a little bit more experience now and knew my way around the airport and how to find the taxi line again. It was earlier this time though, about 8pm. Believe it was Monday night and the poker tour was still going on a Bellagio. So I knew there would still be plenty of action going on. Funny enough, I still had my room available to me for another night. But, I lost the key at this point again. So I went to the front desk and gave her some speech and she handed me a new one. Made the walk with my bag over my shoulder, past the table from the night before and up to my room to drop my bag off and head back downstairs to find some sort of redemption. I pulled out a shot of jack from the fridge and downed that in one breath. I had a nice little buzz to be honest to start off my night.

I headed downstairs and the poker room was somehow more packed than the last time. Highest game they had going was $200/$400 hold em only. There was a $1k nightly about to start and they were getting 350 players a night the floor man said, shooting out a first place prize of about $100k. I decided to head to the tournament room and see how many runners there were so far. There were 290 and registration was going to be open for another hour. The tournament was just starting, so I decided to enter since the waiting list in the poker room was insane.

I ordered a seven and seven at the bar just outside the tournament room and sat down at some random table by the window looking out at the fountain. Keep in mind that tournament poker is way different than cash games. Especially no limit tournaments as opposed to the high stakes limit cash games I was playing. They're about as opposite as you can get. The first place prize of $117k was quite intriguing and motivating though. We were about two hours into it and registration had closed

out at 385 players. I was playing well despite how
drunk I was and had about 100 big blinds with 200
players left. It wasn't necessarily a turbo, but we
only started with $5k in tournament chips and the
levels were 20 minutes long. Maybe fast paced was
a better way to describe it.

Time kept on rolling by and before I knew it we
were down to two tables. The hand that really gave
me the go to chip lead and drive for the remainder
of the tournament was a nail biter for both me and
my opponent. The average was about $85k and I
was sitting on about $145k, blinds were $2k/$4k. It
was folded around to me on the button and I raised
it up with A3 to $9k, the big blind called and the
flop came down 245xxx. I don't remember the suits
but I am pretty certain that there wasn't a flush draw
of any kind. He was the only player at the table that
had more chips than me. He bet out $15k into my
flopped straight which is also called a wheel and I
decided to just call. The turn was a jack, an
irrelevant card and he put out $30k this time. I sat
there for a few moments trying to maybe represent
an A5 kind of a hand and decided to go all in. He
snap called and I was almost worried he had the
higher straight. He was shell shocked when I said
wheel and he flipped over his set of 2s. With one
card to come I was praying the board didn't pair.

The river was a king.

Phew, scoop! Won that monster and was now
sitting on about $300k. I ordered another drink and
a shot of jack and we were almost down to 12
players. We took a short break and came back. It
was coming up on four in the morning by the time
we reached the final table. The average was about

$175k and I had chipped up a little more and knocked out the last two players, so I was sitting with more than double the average with close to $400k. I was going to win this fucking thing, I knew it. That was also one of the coolest attributes I had established at this point in my career. Prediction and just knowing that on that certain day I was going to win. I would be on my way to cash games and I just knew heading in that I was going to win that day. And it never failed me I don't think. Sitting here at this final table as relaxed and drunk as I was, with this chip lead, this tournament was mine along with the $117k first place prize.

Before I realized it, I could barely stack my own chips anymore. At the same time, it was a tournament and they couldn't just kick me out and cash me out and tell me to leave because of how intoxicated I was. The gracious floor man sat down next to me and guided me along. He would help me stack my chips and let me know when it was my turn too. The hands I wasn't involved in, I started to doze off and he would nudge me and wake me up. I was instantly exhausted and ruining the moment I was in. It was six in the morning at this point and there was still a crowd of about thirty spectators watching us. We were up on the stage and the chairs that were vacant had been removed from the table. I finally woke up a little bit more and asked for an energy drink and a salad of some type. We were still three handed and guaranteed $55k.

I had about $900k and the blinds were $15k/$30k. The short stack went all in for $200k with A7, I peeled back AJ and called. I flopped a jack and it was about over. We went in to heads up and I had him out stacked about 2-1. We only played 5 hands or so heads up. I had K8 and min-raised, he called with J8 and the flop miraculously panned out as 842. We got it all in and that was about it, I had won and that was pretty much the last thing I remembered from the night.

I woke up the following morning very confused. I had blacked out and was worried I had done something stupid. It was almost four in the afternoon as the clock had read and I had been asleep about nine hours. I didn't see any cash or chips on my night stand and instantly wondered where my $117k was. Plus, I had $40k in cash in my jeans that I brought downstairs last night thinking I was going to be playing cash games. I checked the safe next to the bed to at least make sure the $60k I left in the room was still in there, and it was. The second I stood up from my bed I knew I was going to puke. I ran into the bathroom and got sick for about ten minutes. Once it was all out of me, I felt much better. I threw some water on my face and walked out of the bathroom praying I had almost $160k stashed somewhere in my jeans. It was a relief at first when I picked up my jeans and they were heavier than jeans should be. I found the $40k in cash stashed in mates of $10k a piece in each front pocket right where I left them. But $117k in cash would be a little more noticeable if it was there. I reached in the back pocket and felt some chips, six of them to be exact. There were four $25k chips that were purple and called pancakes and two other $5k flags, coming out to $110k. I assumed that I had tipped the floor and the dealers the other $7k that was missing.

What a relief. So, what a night! I screamed in enjoyment! I was ecstatic the money was still kept nestled in my pockets and I had nothing to worry about. I needed a desperate steaming hot shower and would go from there for now.

When I got dressed and headed downstairs to find food, I had to stop in the tournament room assuming the same night shift would be working. Behold there was the same floor man on duty that was helping me out the night before. I walked in and he saw me and he just started laughing at me. He told me that I was quite the handful the night before, but when it was over with I shook everyone's hand and did in fact tip the floor and the dealers out the remaining $7k that I was missing. That was a good feeling. He asked if I was going to play the same tournament again that night and I told him that I missed my cash games, so I was going to find dinner and look to see what was going on in the poker room. We shook hands and went our separate ways.

I figured it would be best to throw my name on a list now and find food so that the time elapses. The highest game that was going was $200/$400 and the game was full with a couple of names on the list. I threw my name on it and went to the café for dinner. I left the $100k in cash that I brought up in the safe in my room and just carried around the $110k I had in chips from the tournament for convenience. When I was finally finished with dinner, I figured that I would look into seeing if I was able to get a security box located at one of the cages so that I didn't have to keep on carrying around so much money in my pockets. They were available and I decided to get one. It was cool because you could cash in like $300k in cash if you wanted to and they could simply divert them into just chips and you could store it in your box. It costs $100 a month and was insanely convenient for traveling purposes. I decided to go upstairs and get the $100k in cash and also put it in there. I kept $60k, two $25k chips and $10k in cash. Threw the other $150k or so in the box and handed it back to the lady in the cage.

I headed towards the bar and grabbed a long island. After the size of the steak I just ate, I should be content for a while. My seat had literally just opened up when I walked back into the high limit area. I gave the floor man one of the $25ks and told him to bring me $5k in bananas, which are the yellow $1ks and the rest in black $100s. Mark Gregorich was on my right and recognized me from the other day. Steve Sung sat next to the dealer and to complete out the lineup, old school Thor Hansen sat at the end of the table. It was a full game of pros and I was the hottest kid around right now. I sunk in and got comfortable. I was finally at home.

Throughout my back and forth trips from Vegas to Chicago, I would have plenty of back to back trips like this. Win six digits, lose six digits. Filled with long time periods where the time of day didn't exist. Where all of my decisions were made on the drop of a dime and I was gambling with amounts of money that make me sick to think about these days, became my everyday lifestyle. Most of my trips I played in the $40/$80 game up to $200/$400 limit games. But they got as high as $500/$1k sometimes. It really just depended on who was in town that week. I always tried to get a seat in the biggest game that was going on.

I have a thousand more stories about my excursions from Chicago to Vegas, but that is just a couple of them with a few more to come. The town was growing on me, everything about it. I loved the attention I got from the employees, the tourists, women, the smells, free limo rides everywhere and the money I was making. My drinking was getting worse, but I don't think I had a chance of making that go away. My bankroll just crept past $575k and I was nothing but hungry for more.

"I believe that sex is one of the most beautiful, natural, wholesome things that money can and can't buy."

$17k Hooker-

Ten months had passed. Fall was approaching here in Chicago and I was maintaining a different kind of life. It had been a long year of back and forth trips from Chicago to Vegas and down to Champaign to see my friends and Mindy. I was keeping myself more than busy and occupied with life. It was really the same thing every day now that I've had time to reflect on it. Day in and day out the only thing that ever changed really was the amount of money I was either winning or losing. In return, that pretty much defined my success in life too. If that's all I had, that's all I had for now. My drinking was the worse it had ever been, but I didn't fear it as much as a problem since I was winning consistently. I had my nights of losing. But my bankroll was around $750k, so I was up about $200k on the year one way or the other. When you throw in traveling expenses and partying, I probably made twice that amount in 2007. I guess I had nothing to complain about.

The summer was over and I had spent more time in Chicago than expected. I had a girlfriend now that I met at U of I that took up most of my time when I was back home for the last year almost. It took away some time from my boys in Champaign, but they knew that I needed that balance as well and how much she meant to me. In some way, she was my sense of reality. It was hard for me to find a girl that knew about my lifestyle that still wanted to be with me for the right reasons. Money is a sexy and addictive item if you put it in front of some people that aren't used to it. It can make them like you for all of the wrong reasons if you aren't careful enough. Thankfully, I had enough encounters with those people in a thousand different scenarios in Vegas and I was able to identify them early on. They were the scumbags and the weasels that only want you because of the amount of money that you have in front of you. The businessmen that I would sometimes have escorted away from the tables I was playing blackjack at because they wouldn't stop talking to me about business deals and opportunities I could potentially have if I just listened to their story or offer. Who is more important to the casino? The kid with $150k in front of him betting $1k a hand, or the businessman just sitting there with $2,000 betting $150 a hand and harassing one of their customers after he has requested of him numerous amounts of times to leave him alone? Don't even get me started on the hookers either. The ones with a little bit of money in their pockets and a tack of common sense, would actually sit down and play blackjack with you. Rather than just come up from behind you with some story and start rubbing the back of your neck. I would say start rubbing the back of your head, but most of you would assume I was referring to my dick. At least the smart hookers would buy in and bet the minimum amount to strike up a conversation with you and make it seem as if they weren't hookers at first.

The automatic doors opened up from the parking garage and into the airport lobby I walked. It was some time during the week and I had half a bottle of captain and coke that I was trying to finish before I got to security check. I was exhausted. I couldn't remember the last time that 24 hours had gone by where I wasn't intoxicated one way or the other. Since I was doing alright financially, it never dawned on me just how bad my drinking was becoming. I had left the city games drunk, got home and packed a bag, grabbed five shots at the liquor store and made this drink on the way. Luckily enough it was in a 16 oz. coke bottle and camouflaged so that no one realized what I was drinking while I waited in line to buy my ticket for another trip to Vegas. I got to the counter and the lady recognized me.

"Back to Vegas Mr. Woolworth?"

All I could do was smile and laugh, she knew. The next flight available was in three hours, a late one around 8:30. Which was fine with me really, I had no food in my stomach and I could keep on drinking too. I handed over the $250 that a one flight now costs and headed towards security. I chugged as much as I could before I reached the security check that I almost got sick. I could tell that I was a mess and the first thing I planned on doing when I got to my hotel room in Vegas, was to take a long and hot shower. I needed it badly. Just to get the scent of repulsed decisions off my chest and the alcohol exiting through my pores too.

I found some food, had a couple of more drinks and before I knew it we were boarding. Airports to me are such a magical place. You see every type of person there. Seems like they never fly anywhere and you're just the only one that comes and goes. They're running, talking on their phones, laughing, or chasing down their child who now knows how to run instead of walk all of a sudden. They speak tons of different languages and live in a billion different types of lives. I always wondered where they were going or what they were feeling. I wondered if they were happy or sad. Thinking back on the few faces that I can remember I wondered if they were still alive or not.

The captain came on and did his speech when we were about 25 minutes outside of Vegas. It actually had been about a week since I had been back. I was going through a break with Mindy because she traveled to Europe with her best friend for a month. To me, breaks in a relationship were so fucking stupid. If you love me and want to be with me, why do we need a break exactly? So that we can figure ourselves out? Isn't that what being in a relationship is all about? Growing together and figuring things out as a couple? To me it was just an excuse because you either didn't want to be together, or you wanted to fuck someone else and not get in trouble for it. And use the break as an excuse to support an argument down the road that I didn't want to be a part of. She had been in Europe now for about four weeks and was supposed to be home within the next week so that she could get back to U of I for her senior year. We had been messaging each other back and forth while she was gone and we knew we missed each other. I was still disturbed with the timing of her wanting to go on a break just before she went to Europe. It didn't make a lot of sense to me. I wanted to keep my guard up or whatever you wanted to call it. But I was crazy about her at the same time.

I didn't have much feeling when it came to other women. At least I can admit that now. I had lost the thought of caring really. I was an asshole to a majority of the people that I came in contact with because of how cocky the game and fortune was turning me into. When I think about it today, I just want to hug anyone from back then and apologize to them over and over for the way I treated them. It truly breaks my heart these days thinking I said and did some of the things that I did back then. The only way that I can change any of those thoughts now, is by giving respect to everyone that I come in contact with on daily basis from here on out. I would like to think that I have become that guy right now, this second. Now my conversations are filled with courtesy and respect. A simple please and thank you goes such a long way with every conversation you can come encounter with each and every day.

But women are beautiful creatures. They're the sexiest thing on this planet. But in Vegas, they were just statues to me. None of them really mattered. Either they were there on bachelorette parties and would be headed back to their respectable cities in a couple of days, or they were waitresses with fake tits that got hit on a hundred times a day and you were just another bird in the mix. Or they were constant alcoholics, coke heads and strippers, I could go on really. It was truly hard just to meet a girl in Vegas that didn't fall into one of those categories and actually had a respectable career that I could bring home to my mother with appreciation.

I got comped a 2,500 square foot suite at Bellagio for a few nights. I honestly couldn't remember the last time that I had paid for a room in the last six months. Since I had acquired a dangerous yet profitable blackjack addiction, paying for anything in Vegas became extinct to me. $300 dinners, shows, penthouse suites, buffets, limos and all of the rest came straight out of the casinos pocket. If I was ever pulling money out of my pocket it was to gamble with. The suites at Bellagio were like little castles. Some of them were two stories tall, but even if they were one story, the windows were still from the floor to ceiling and cathedral ceilings they were. Everything was marble, the views were out of this world and you felt like you were a king. I wish I had spent more time in some of those rooms. But, I really only used them to sleep in.

I kept my partying to a minimum out in Vegas and saved it for Champaign. Granted I was intoxicated every day, that was really just my way to keep myself fueled and motivated. The money was becoming dull to me. It makes me laugh now that I can admit that at some moments in my career, I actually got bored with what I was doing. It was like I needed more of a challenge somehow, just something. I couldn't come up with anything. I was actually getting bored making $20k a day or losing it too. It was just an almost irrelevant feeling to me by this point to some stature. Maybe I needed to play higher stakes to test myself, but I didn't want to go on some awful losing streak where I found it impossible to move back down in limits because I would feel as if that sum of money wasn't worth it anymore. I didn't understand the value of the dollar or how much I was truly making compared to that of an ordinary working civilian. I had gotten into such a rhythm of winning that I almost lost that passion of getting back on my feet after a losing session. Whether it was from poker or blackjack, I kind of lost that feeling of caring that I was winning. I don't think I can even really blame it on anything. Everything about Vegas had just kind of grown on me.

72 hours later I was waking up from a long nights sleep. Something that was quite rare for me being in Vegas. Usually I could never sleep longer than a handful of hours in that town. Didn't matter if I was up for two days straight or not, a few hours of rest could have me entirely recharged for another 48 hours of gambling. I had so much energy somehow still, that I had to get back down there and keep pushing and keep learning and keep living this dream.

It was a quiet trip really. I was playing primarily $100/$200 for the last few days. I was up somewhere around $12k or so over three sessions. I decided that I would order some room service after I showered and make it an easy night. Maybe just lie around or throw $10k on a game and watch it and drink. I had plans of flying out the following morning so that I could get home and see my family and friends. After room service came and went, I got the itch to play some poker. I made a call down to the poker room and the $100/$200 game was still going on. It was five handed which was my favorite and I told them I would be down shortly.

I threw $10k on the table, which was pretty much my profit for the trip these last few days. Not all of my trips back then were entirely out of control. Mixed in with $100k swings and binging for 48 hours straight, sometimes I did have relaxing trips such as this. Sure, to the normal human a relaxing trip to Vegas was a martini next to the pool followed by a tasty dinner and a walk down the strip. For me, a few balanced days of high stakes poker and no blackjack was as laid back as I could get at this point in my career.

I had a 16 oz. steak and some grilled shrimp in my stomach, so I was good to go for a little while. I ordered a long island from one of the sexiest waitresses the Bellagio had to offer and got to work. It had been almost five weeks since I had sex. When you go from having sex whenever you wanted, to nothing, I was practically dying. Then when you mix in money and intoxication too, the awful decisions that I had to neglect in that town constantly were exhausting. I didn't want to cheat on her. But I didn't know if we were getting back together when she got home from Europe either. And if there is ever a place to be horny and helpless at some points, it's Vegas.

I killed the game in four hours for about $10k. I love me some short-handed limit cash games. It was midnight or so and I figured that I would take the $20k I was up for this trip over to the blackjack table and see what I could do with it for a couple of hours. I pounded about four long islands while I was playing poker, so I wasn't speaking much English at this point. I want to say that it was a Monday night too, so the casino and pit itself wasn't packed at all. For anyone that doesn't know what the pit is, it's the cluster fuck of blackjack tables and craps tables. Any other table game that the devil established. Why it is called that I am not sure of, but I am sure everyone can define it through their own terms.

I tossed her two of the $5k flags and placed the other two next to my drink. The blackjack tables were lit up with a bright and intense ray of heat and the rest of the casino was always dark. I liked sitting directly across from the blackjack dealer so that I felt like it was a heads up battle. I usually always tried to sit down at high stakes tables so that no one else would sit down while I was playing and mess up a rhythm I may have or a streak of winning I was on. It was always exhausting and became a tutorial session if a couple of tourists sat down just to bet the minimum and my next determination was based off of their mistakes and poor decisions from lack of knowledge for the game of blackjack. But! I had recently just purchased a 49mm Breitling with 99 diamonds eclipsing the bezel. It was the first watch

I had ever purchased and it's amazing the amount of attention that you can receive from it. Of course, given my age and the fact that I looked unhealthy and was 130 pounds, most people outside of Vegas assumed it was a fake piece. It showed a sign of respect amongst poker players and floor men alike that knew me and knew the stakes I was playing every day. The band was a gator brown design and the head of it was steel with a blue face. It was probably the sexiest watch I ever had owned and rightfully so when you throw in the $23k price tag. It seemed like everyone had a watch in that town. I became obsessed with them and at one point my watch collection was somewhere valued around $90k.

I sat down with $20k which was usually an average buy in for me when it came to blackjack. I actually wasn't in the high stakes area just past the lobby on the right, I was more so towards the last pit on the outer edge by the slot machines. Since it was late and I knew that they would be shutting this pit down soon based off of lack of action, I asked the floor man if it was ok that we make this a $500 minimum bet table and to leave it open. He made a call to his boys upstairs and eventually gave me the thumbs up. My primary reason for that decision was because these decks were being handled by automatic shufflers. Rather than by the two deck shoes or regular six deck shoes I had to sit through in the high limit pits. In the end that would result in more hands being dealt to me and a chance to win more money throughout the course of the night. To some people this is an absurd request since the house obviously has an edge on you. But, when you are a degenerate and live in a fearless mind that I had built inside of me, this seemed like a walk in the park. I was up about $14k really quick until the next fuck job happened. I had just won three or four hands in a row of betting $1k to $1,500 and decided to throw a $5k flag out in the box. She dealt me two 4s against her 6 and I decided to split them and threw out another $5k to the other 4. She gave me a 6 and I opted to double down on it for another $5k and she panned out a king, giving me 20. Not bad so far. On the other 4 she gave me an 8 for a sum of 12 and I decided to waive it off. So if she busts, I had $30k coming back my way. She pulled out a 4 to give her ten and then an ace to make her scoop me with a beautiful 21. She picked up my $15k in front of me and I was down $1k for this session. I was annoyed and bet the $1k I was in the hole with, she dealt me blackjack of course and I decided to walk away being up $500.

Blackjack can be quite the funny game sometimes. Odds are odds, but most of the time the percentages don't go your way. But man, when they do, you can win a fortune.

As I was walking back to my room, all I could think about was sex. Every girl that walked past me was insanely hot and I just wanted to hit on all of them. I couldn't really walk a straight line at this point either. Chances are I would be pretty useless in bed. I finally staggered up to my suite and crashed into bed. Laying there exhausted and helpless, missing Mindy a lot that I was on a break with and going on five weeks of not having sex, I was finally desperate.

"Alright."

I kind of said it out loud and in disgust to myself, so I rolled over and opened the drawer next to my bed and pulled out the yellow pages. Found the entertainment and escort section, closed my eyes and picked a company. I gave them a call and it was like walking down a buffet line. You could pick a girl of any race, age, breast size, weight, hair color and they would have her sent to you in 45 minutes. When she arrived you apparently had the option of rejecting her if you weren't satisfied with her appearance no questions asked. I ordered a blonde in her 20's, busty and skinny.

"Ok, sir. She will be there in 45 minutes. What's your room number?"

I was nervous as fuck when I hung up the phone. I didn't know what to expect or how much she was going to cost. I threw about $40k in my safe in my other room and left about $2k in my pocket. I figured that this chick couldn't cost me anymore than that really. I had a little bit of time and opened up my bar and made myself a drink and pulled up one of the chairs next to the windows and opened up the curtains to watch over the strip until she got here. I was actually looking forward to this.

I could hear my ice start to rub up against the glass of the second drink I had made myself and before I knew it, over an hour had passed. I was getting anxious and curious if I maybe gave the lady on the phone the wrong room number. I called her back and told her that the girl still hadn't arrived. She told me that she would call me back in a few minutes and let me know where she is at. The phone rang about ten minutes later and they said that they called her three times and that she isn't answering.

"We're extremely sorry about this sir. Do you want us to send you another girl for half the price?"

"Actually, no it's ok. I'm not really feeling it anymore. Thanks though."

And I hung up. So there I was being stood up by a fucking hooker. Talk about rock bottom depression. To this day I still wonder what happened to her and if she was alright. Or if I had actually given the lady the wrong room number. We would never be able to confirm that either since she couldn't get ahold of her when she called her back. But, life goes on.

It was about two in the morning by this point and I had just caught some gust of energy and figured I would go back downstairs and just gamble until I had to leave for the airport in a few hours. The poker room was finally dead and the $100/$200 game had finally ended as well. The highest limit going on was $15/$30 and I would literally fall asleep if I sat down in a game that small right now. I turned around and headed back to the pits and to one of the few open blackjack tables. I ordered another drink and bought in for $20k again. Déjà vu.

Three hours would pass the clock, three more long islands would run through me and I had $3,400 left in front of me. I decided it was time to call it a night and end my trip up $3k. I threw the dealer a $300 tip and Mikey the floor man the other $100 and walked towards the cage down $17k for the session.

So, if the hooker shows up, I fuck her and it costs me maybe $400 and I go to sleep until I have to leave for the airport. Instead, she never arrives at my doorstep, so I go back downstairs and lose $17k in three hours playing blackjack. Symbolically she's been named the $17k Hooker to me.

Completely numb to my loss, I threw the remaining $20k into my box at the cage and pocketed $5k in cash for the week I was going to be back in Chicago. Over the course of the last year I had merged all of my money out here to Vegas and in several different security boxes in three different casinos. Then I would just bring back a few grand with me to Chicago for pocket cash when needed.

To this day, I am sure there are plenty of people that don't believe me that I never paid for sex in all of those times that I was out in Vegas. But, because of her I can hold my head high and still say that I never did. It does nothing but make me disgusted with myself that the thought even crossed my mind that night though. Hormones win most of the time I guess.

So, thanks $17k Hooker. You gave my morals a reason to live.

"You have to walk on that edge where it hurts a little bit if you lose. And it just makes every day in your life exciting. It's not boring at all. I think that's why I still love to do it."

A Legend-

Growing up I loved baseball. I always wanted to be a professional baseball player. The thought of being famous just seemed like the way to go in life. Travel all over the country, stay in hotels, money, women and just fame in general was very intriguing to me. I didn't want to just be another ordinary person in life. I wanted to be somebody. So naturally, I looked at all the baseball greats as heroes to me. I wanted to have some kid or inspiring individual to look up to me the same way that I did to them so many years ago. The greats, the heroes and the legends are the entities to what shapes a sport or a certain profession. It gives everyone else something to look forward to and bars to set to strive further in a career. Setting goals and working for them each and every day is something I never considered during my gambling career, I just woke up and did whatever I wanted. That's definitely one thing that still upsets me to this day that I never had a long term plan as to what I was doing and that was definitely an ingredient to my finale.

It was the end of November in 2007 and I had just turned 22 years old. Mindy and I had never been better. She came home from Europe and it was like we were starting from where we left off. We had plenty of long substantial conversations about anything we could talk about at such a young age. My problem was, was that I thought that I had it all figured out. I was living on my own, had a striving career from what I could see, people looked up to the poker player I had become, I had great friends, a loveable girlfriend and my parents were my best friends. How can life get any better? Only way I could find out was by waking up tomorrow and seeing what the day had to offer.

It was a Thursday afternoon and was quite gorgeous down in Champaign. Maybe in the 40's and sunny and just warm enough where we could walk to one of the local sub shops for a lunch before I headed back to the airport in Chicago and back to Vegas for a few days. Sometimes these moments meant more to me than anything I ever did back then. It was always a nice little vacation going down to U of I. It was like I kind of had it all on backwards. I went to

Vegas for work and U of I for vacation. But being able to grab a quick lunch with someone that means the world to me was the moments I tried to value back then, more than anything I ever did back in Vegas. We ate, spent some time together and before I knew it I was back in my car and headed back to the airport.

Life was alright. My parents and I were good. They were coming along the more I did what I did and I still tried to call them every day with updates on what was going on. I had my moments where even in the midst of my success, that their phone would ring at three in the morning. It would be me on the other line crying. Just because it looked like I was the happiest guy on the planet, didn't mean that I wasn't dying inside on some days. I was quite lonely out there and just in general I always wondered if what I was doing with my life was the correct route to take. Over the last three years of doing this I had plenty of people laugh at me, mock me and just be straight rude to my profession. Whether it was during a conversation with a stranger at an airport, friends through social media or even random people in general, criticism was something I faced on a daily basis. I knew that if this was something I planned on continuing, that I would have to take the critics in with the rest of them and handle it how I wanted to. By winning and continuing on in life with how I want to live it. That is definitely one piece of advice I will give my children. Simply surround yourself with people you want to be around. Whatever the case may be and with that constructed element you have designed, you'll find happiness in anything that you do in life. It may take a while, but it's worth the wait.

My sixth drink of the flight was almost finished and just in time for me to see the lights of the outer boundaries of Vegas starting to cascade across my window. I got used to a lot of things in Vegas. I didn't overly stare at hot girls anymore, the money was like I was playing with pennies and the world just seemed to go by me as I walked down the strip or through lobbies. Everyone would be pointing and taking pictures in groups, just as happy as could be since they booked their trips months in advance. I would just look ahead and continue on with my destination with my gym bag over my shoulder. Living my own life how I wanted to. There was something about every landing coming into Vegas that I always had to stare out the window like I was some little kid again. And for that few minutes or so before we landed, I remembered why I was doing what I was doing. Because not many others are getting the opportunity that I am.

I went off the week before at Caesars and lost about $80k playing blackjack, so I knew that I had free rooms available there. I stayed in three different hotels usually. How I decided where I was staying for that trip was really made when I got to the cab line. I either stayed at Bellagio, Caesars or upwards on the strip at the Wynn.

"Caesars please."

The cabbie looked like he was just a kid, but we took the highway route and arrived at the circle driveway within twenty minutes. I was able to get a nice suite somewhere around the 20th floor I think. Bellagio to me will always have the nicest suites, but they were all beautiful in the end. They all had their own little specs and luxurious ways that even to me I would say wow when I walked into the room for the first time. This one actually had a hot tub in the living room floor, full bar and steel kitchen. If you wanted, you could have a butler come up and cook you whatever meal that you craved. Or if you wanted to have a party, you could have a bartender of your choice come up and host your party for you. The windows were just like every other suite and went from the floor to the ceiling. The fruit basket still had wet fruits in them since they had just been washed and a six pack of my favorite energy drink sat in a bucket with ice in it on the counter of the kitchen. Before you were allowed to go up to your room sometimes, they would ask for thirty minutes or so to prep for it for you. They did it right in Vegas.

The weekend was here apparently. It never really made a difference to me other than more people in the pits and on the strip. Capacity of the poker room never really varied unless there was a tournament in town. If there wasn't, it was pretty much the same traffic all the time. I was on a mission for each trip to try out new restaurants all over town. It was in my full advantage that I could try dishes that not a lot of other people could. And I love food to the bone. There aren't a whole lot of better things in this world than delicious dinners and to die for desserts. This town had plenty of options too. My latest obsession was fish and sushi and everything in between. I tried to divert from so much room service and actually take time out to go out to dinners. Only downfall was that if I couldn't find one of my poker buddies to come with, I was going out alone. Granted though, every five star restaurant out there had a bar to sit at. I had plenty of dates I went on all alone. I am glad and happy with myself today that I took advantage of that opportunity. I had dishes at the most elegant restaurants Vegas had to offer every night going forward. It was a kick of balance to my lifestyle. To make it a priority, get dressed and make sure that it happened. It was a good way to start my nights and head to the poker table with a full stomach. Rather than me just ordering room service to the table and taking away concentration from the game, my newly premeditated arrangement was a favorable scenario for me.

Waking up Saturday night from my session the night before was something I wanted to forget. I got absolutely destroyed. Something that I wasn't used to playing high stakes cash games, usually all of my big losses came from playing blackjack. This one definitely hit home to me when I rolled out of bed and into the shower. Only good thing is that when big games like that get off on Friday nights, they were always going to be either getting off again Saturday night or they were still going on from the night before. Being as competitive as I am, I had to jump in the game. We were playing a ten game mix with seven limit games and then 2-7 NL single draw, NL hold em and pot limit Omaha. We were playing $400/$800 limits and $100/$200 for the other three games. I played for about 15 hours Friday night after dinner and on into Saturday afternoon and ended up losing about $130k. It was my largest loss to date, including blackjack. It had been an awful month for me really. I was down somewhere around $225k and my bankroll was just a hair above half a million. I knew that when I went downstairs tonight to get back into that game, I needed to be extra focused and only drink regular well drinks, not martinis or long islands out of tolerance of being an alcoholic.

I grabbed dinner at one of Vegas' finest steakhouses located inside Caesars. I liked the new routine I had going on, and I didn't want my recent losing streak to interfere with it. I knew that I would pull out of this funk that I was in and everything would go back to how it was. I called the poker room over at Bellagio when I was paying for my tab and the game was larger than the night before. There were two tables going now, one was the one I was playing in the night before and the other was the same games, but $500/$1k limits and $100/$200 still for the NL games. I said to throw me on the list. I grabbed a jack and coke outside of the restaurant at a random bar and made the walk on over to Bellagio. It was a nice chilly night in the 50s and this walk was going to be the most peaceful two minutes for the entire trip probably, so I embraced it. I could deal with the fact of losing. I understood it. It happens and I hated it, since I was working for the money that lay in front of me. The best part about it was that there is always going to be another opportunity the following day if you do it correctly and I was ready for that moment. I stopped at the cage by the pits and pulled out $200k from my box and made my way to the poker room. I just didn't want to get ahead of myself and feel like I needed to make back all $130k and then some. My goal was $100k, make that and walk away for the session.

The chips bounced around in my pocket as I walked into the poker room and up to the high stakes area. The $500/$1k game was six handed and looked like a dream come true. I knew all of the players and

knew I could win in this game. Half of them were
drinking wine and there was probably over $1
million dollars on the table between the six of them.
They welcomed me and we got caught up on the
night before. A couple of the other guys at the table
next to me were still playing from the night before
and it showed as well. I bought in for $100k and got
another drink. Game on.

The first decent sized hand I got involved in was
Pot Limit Omaha. For anyone that doesn't know
PLO, it's the same as hold em, except you get four
cards instead of two. But, you have to and can only
use two of the four cards to make your best five
card hand. I was up $4k early on from a couple of
hands, and then I got dealt AdAhQd9c. Suited aces
with some high cards always deserved a raise pre
flop, so I repotted the open raiser to $2,200 and got
called in three spots. The flop was beautiful, panned
out KJT, with the "T" being a ten. So I had flopped
broadway, or the ace high straight. It was checked
around to me and I threw out $7,500, got called by
the player behind me and a well-known pro raised it
to $27k. It was back to me and he had about $45k
behind him. The player that just called behind me
had about $300k in front of him though. I was
worried if I repotted it and he went all in, he would
have a set and I could lose everything in front of me
if it didn't go my way. I was hoping that the player
that made it $27k had Q9 for the smaller straight
since I already had two of the aces. I decided to
raise the pot to $85k and the player behind me
folded. The original raiser called off his remaining
$45k and we flipped up our hands. The pot in front
of us was roughly $160k and he revealed JJ23 for a
set of jacks. As long as the board didn't pair to give

him a full house, I was in the clear. It came out as a six and a seven and I ended up with the nuts and the winner. I scooped up the chips and added them to my stack and tipped the dealer a few hundred bucks. Just thirty minutes into the session I was up about $100k. I know that I said that I would get up and leave if I hit that number, but I obviously didn't plan on winning it all that quickly either. It is also awful etiquette in the poker world to do what is called a hit and run, to win extremely early and get up and leave. So, I stayed put.

Before I knew it we were playing heads up and I was up about $175k for the session. He was a well-known player that I had played with plenty of times. He was down about $250k and I didn't want to just leave him hanging. I know what that's like and I didn't want to be that asshole. He and I played heads up for about two more hours until he finally called it a night, somewhere around four in the morning on Sunday. I won $185k and couldn't be happier. That's one thing I remember doing a lot of back in my poker career. It was like, if I had to win for whatever reason, I always did. My determination was unlike anything I had ever seen before even to this day. When I needed to get the job done, I always did. By the time I chatted with some players that were still playing in another game, dropped off the $380k to my box at the cage and made my way back across the street and over to Caesars, the sun was coming up. I was absolutely starving, so I made a drink when I got back up to my room and ordered some steak and eggs and fruit. Pulled back the panoramic curtains and dragged the couch over by one of the windows to watch the sun come up and threw my feet up onto the glass. It was quite a tranquil moment and I am glad that I still remember what it felt like. It was moments like that that haven't died yet from my memory. I can still feel the heat through the glass, the feeling of the whiskey headed down inside of me and just the purity feeling of a successful night. My breakfast arrived and I dove in and eventually fell asleep. Today was a good day.

I woke up around noon and didn't have any energy really to gamble at those kinds of stakes today. I assumed there would be at least one game of that size going on at some point today, but yesterday was stressful. Whether I won almost $200k or not, I kind of wanted to just play and be relaxed and drink. Not worry about what game we were on either. That's the hardest part when playing mixed cash games and drinking. If you aren't paying full attention you can literally forget what game you are playing and it can cost you thousands. I was up about $50k for the trip and had planned on flying out tomorrow afternoon, stop back at home for a day to see my parents and then head back down to U of I. I had a fruit salad in my fridge that I had yet to eat and it looked perfect for a morning such as this. I decided to do things a little differently today and take my time with the rest of life. I put some music on, popped open the fruit salad, made myself a vodka on the rocks and jumped into my hot tub ass naked that lay perfectly in the middle of my front room. Just kind of sat there and enjoyed the view of the strip and the mountains and finished my drink and salad and hopped into the shower.

I went on a small shopping spree and bought about $2k worth of clothes downstairs at the mall. To the point where I actually had to buy another suitcase just to make sure that all of it made it back to Chicago. By the time I got back to my room it was about dinner time. I picked out a new outfit that I had just bought and made my way over to Bellagio and picked out a restaurant. After dinner was over with, I grabbed a drink at the piano bar, stopped at the cage and grabbed the $50k I was up for the last few days and made my way to the poker room.

The poker room was quite empty for being a Sunday night. Thankfully enough the $100/$200 game was seven handed with two open seats and I made my way over there. I bought in for $5k and was looking for a laid back evening. I ordered a long island and was dealt my first hand before I even had chips out in front of me. One of the regulars gave me $1k in the meantime until the floor man came back with my racks. First hand I posted and was dealt 9s. I two bet it to $200 and was called by three players. The flop came out 554 and was checked to me and I bet. Both players to my left folded and the player on the button would raise it to $200, I three bet to $300 and he called. The turn was a 6 and I bet again, he raised me to $400 and I called. The river was a 5, giving me 5s full of 9s and I bet out. He called, I flipped over my 9s and he mucked and I scooped my first hand and the $2500 pot. Not a bad way to start off the evening.

The night was more of that same action and everything seemed to be panning out my way. I was up about $9k around two in the morning and getting hungry. The action was dying out and I decided to call it a night. I had a huge taste for chicken tenders, so I opted to order room service and I would just wait for it in the poker room. I ordered another drink and sat at an empty poker table and waited for the food to arrive over by the cage area.

As I was waiting, I looked up from a magazine I was reading and saw a familiar face walk into the poker room at an awfully odd time without Bobby's Room going. It was Chip Reese. For anyone that doesn't know Chip, he is the ultimate of legends when it came to the game of poker. He only played the biggest of games and had been around for over thirty years doing so. He played the game out of heart and respect, not for fame and fortune. Even though he always played in the world's biggest games, he did it like nothing was any different than the little games he would play in downtown Las Vegas thirty years prior. He was the elite of elite, even to this day.

He walked over to the cashier next to me and was just getting off the phone with someone. We had played together in Bobby's Room a couple of times, but at separate tables. I had never sat down with him before. It had always been a dream of mine just to be in a hand with him, to see what it would feel like. To this day I am not too sure what overcame me or how I found the sudden urge to get up off my chair and go talk to him. Maybe it was the curiousness as to what a conversation with him may be like, or maybe it was the alcohol.

"Chip! What brings you here at these hours of the morning with no game going on?"

He looked at me like I was a drunk homeless man for about five seconds and then he recognized me.

"Didn't we play together a couple of months ago?"

"Yes sir! Not at the same table, but in Bobby's Room. Why are you here so late?"

Long story short, he said that he and a friend were supposed to meet there around this time to play some heads up Chinese poker. But as he was walking in from the valet, his buddy called him back and let him know that he wouldn't be able to make it. While he was here he wanted to check on some things that were in his box and here he was waiting for the cashier lady.

So my star struck ass spoke up.

"If you want, I'll play Chinese with you?"

He must have been in a gambling mood because he agreed and we made our way into Bobby's Room. In all honesty when it comes to the poker world, this is entirely similar to going back in time and playing catch with Babe Ruth at Yankee Stadium on national television. I was finally nervous. It was just unreal what was about to happen and we hadn't even gotten our chips yet. First we had to let the floor managers know to open the room up, to supply us with a dealer and get us chips, put it up on the message board that the game was going and then we could begin. We sat across from each other at an empty table in Bobby's Room and he laughed and asked me what my name even was. We finally shook hands and in walked our dealer with a few racks of chips.

We both decided to buy in for $30k and play for $200 a point. Chinese poker if you aren't familiar with it, you get dealt 13 cards. You make your best two five card hands and your best three card hand, totaling out to 13 cards. At the same time as you are finished assembling them, you place them in three layers like a pyramid kind of. Putting your best five card hand on the bottom, second best in the middle and then your three card hand would go on top, always being the worst hand. Since we were going to be playing heads up, we could each receive two hands at once since 13x4 is 52 total cards. It would work out perfectly. We agreed to play two hours minimum and got started.

The next eight hours or so were possibly the best moments that I ever spent in Vegas or in my poker career. We ordered food and drank wine, we talked the whole time and it felt like we were best friends. He was interested in what it was like being an up and coming poker player now, compared to when he was my age thirty years ago and starting out with his career. The poker boom had given birth to millions of people that wanted to play poker for a living and since the internet was hotter than ever, players were developing thousands of different ways to play the game. He said that he just laughs when he turns on the television and he sees some kid with sunglasses and headphones on.

"That's not poker. That's just what the media has made it out to be. Now you have all of these idiots running around trying to be that guy, that exhausting image. Poker is about sitting there drinking a drink and staring your opponent directly in the face when you have a bet out there and you know you're bluffing and you still get him to fold. Poker is about discovering yourself, not hiding yourself behind certain objects."

I couldn't have agreed with him more. I told him all about the career I had thus far and he gave me both advice and criticism. Told him about this past weekend and he made me realize how large of a swing that is given my bankroll. That it could have totally gone the other way and I could be in a bad spot right now for my career. He suggested a few things to me. That if I don't live here in Vegas, to stop coming here so often. To maybe change things up and make Vegas a once a month stop. That I should venture out to other locations that also offered high stakes action if I wanted to continue playing cash games. Such as Tunica, LA or Atlantic City and that it was perfectly alright to always change up the scenery. He was correct, I had done nothing but gone back and forth from Chicago to Vegas for the last 13 months that I wasn't even traveling really. Then came his biggest piece of advice, to play tournaments. Get away from the cash games as often and to use them as a treat or celebration to a big score. There were new tournaments that were being offered all over the world and new tours were being established. He found it to be an amazing time and opportunity to travel as much as I could and to start playing tournaments all over the country. You lose the stress of dealing with high stakes cash games every day, also you would know how much you're winning and losing every day. Not too many things would be a question anymore and the prizes were unbelievable. You could put up $10k for a tournament and win $1.5 million in some of them, or more. If I sit down in a cash game with $10k, the most I may win is $20k-$100k depending on the game.

I had never really thought about all of that, but he truly was correct. Sure, I had some success playing tournaments, but I didn't really know much about them. The largest tournament I had played in up to that point was that $1k buy in I won at Bellagio for $117k, but I went straight back to cash games after that. I wanted to definitely reconstruct my career and lifestyle when I got back to Chicago in the next 24 hours, I had plans to set up a tour schedule and get on the road. I was bored with Vegas and the timing of all of this just felt perfect.

About ten in the morning rolled around and it felt like we had been sitting there for weeks talking and discussing about life and the game. He told me all about his kids and Vegas in the 1970s and what this life was like before the poker boom. He was by far one of the most interesting, honest and inspiring individuals I had ever met. We ordered breakfast and were almost finished with all of it. We decided to call it quits for the session, I was up $2,800. Part of me wanted to give it back to him like I just had a life lesson and a memory that I will never forget for as long as I live. We racked up our chips and brought them over to the cage, colored up to larger denominations and threw them into our respectable security boxes. The exit out to Caesars was past the valet exit, so we took a stroll exit out of Bellagio. We got to the doors leading out to the side driveway and he shook my hand.

"I really hope that you take something away from everything we just talked about in there. I can tell you have some talent and are passionate about this game. Just remember that everything about poker doesn't live back in that room in the high stakes world. The important things in life are what define who you are as a person, and then who you are as a poker player. Never forget that."

And he left.

It was Monday morning and I was dead exhausted. Even though that session was as laid back as it can get, the amount of intensity it had was more draining than anything I had been through. Even the best of the best and household names may have never had a chance to just sit there with literally the best player in the history of the game and take in advice that he may not give to just anyone. It was an experience that I would never forget or ever take for granted. I watched him through the revolving doors as he got into his car and drove down the circle driveway and out of sight.

I was excited to get back to Chicago tonight and put some things together to start traveling around the country to play tournaments and take in a new lifestyle. I would have to predetermine destinations and hotel reservations and everything else that comes along with traveling. It would give me a chance to explore some and not quarantine myself in Vegas anymore.

I arrived home late that night and decided to unpack and get started on everything in the morning. This was before smart phones and the phone I had didn't have great internet access, so I couldn't really look up where all of the tours were in the coming few weeks. I had to wait until I got home and onto the computer. I turned the television off and fell asleep.

Tuesday morning came rather quickly and I was up throughout the night. I was surprised that I didn't just sleep until the sun came up and jump on the computer to put together a schedule for myself, I was really excited. I rolled out of bed around noon and got caught up with my mom a little bit. I filled her in about this past trip and some other life events that were going on. I asked her what she thought about my new idea about traveling and she was all for it and looked at it as a good opportunity as well. I got some paperwork together and made my way over to the computer and logged on to cardplayer.com to find all of the schedules for all of the tournaments going on around the country.

"Chip Reese 1951-2007"

The top headline had read just that. Chip had died. I was just with him 28 hours before and apparently that night after we shook hands and spent our memorable session together, he died in his home and in his sleep from the effects of pneumonia. I never even noticed that anything was wrong with him. He was all full of laughs and a good gracious guy, open to sharing his stories and advertising advice about anything. Unless he put in a last second session in a few hours later for whatever reason, chances are I am the last person that ever had the fascinated chance of sitting across the table from him. I always hold that possibility to my heart and because of what he said to me before he left that day in the lobby, I always cherished it to myself and my love for the game. I felt like some type of invisible torch had been passed along to me from him and it was now my job to carry it. I was instantly in tears sitting at my computer table. I was entirely shell shocked and didn't know how to react or anything. I had just told my mother this story about my past few days in Vegas and when she walked past me and saw me crying, all I could do was point at the screen and let her read it for herself.

That few hours that I got to spend with a true legend of the game would change the next few months of my career. I can't ever thank him enough for taking out the time to spend with me that he did. I was nothing but a drunk stranger with some cash and a request if he wanted to play heads up. He could have easily said no and returned home for his final hours, but he didn't.

I felt like I had work to do. I felt as if maybe he knew he was going to die and he wanted to change one last person's outlook on life somehow and that's why he agreed to play heads up with me in Bobby's Room. I needed to plan out a schedule and get on the road and see if I could fulfill his wishes.

If it means anything, legends never die. And I will remember that moment with him forever.

"I waited my whole life to be recognized in public by complete strangers. But over time I regretted ever wanting that responsibility in the first place."

Fame-

Respect and fame are two completely different things. I was used to the respect that I had received everywhere I had gone from my peers, house games, to Shakopee, to the underground games, family, friends at U of I, and the regular gamblers and floor men in Vegas all over the strip. I was used to them complimenting me and asking me questions about the game. Or shooting me that random look when I would win some huge hand or make an unbelievable call and wonder how I did what I just did. Heart and passion and love for the game were the answers I would usually throw out there, but just in different definitions. It was really the only natural high that I had left. I had plenty of people tell me before I was becoming publicly known about the talent I had acquired not just for poker, but for gin rummy, chess and blackjack. The way I carried myself and the surprised hands I would show the table sometimes. The way I bet my chips and how I never showed any emotion playing the stakes that I was playing. That so many players in such a little amount of time had come and gone and I was still around, playing in games that made so many players go broke. That if anyone was ever going to make it out of Chicago and win some phenomenal immense tournament it was going to be me. I had taken on a lot of responsibility with being pursued as the best in Chicago at such a young age. Like a meager representative.

I was still trying to finish my cereal after I read the top headline that Chip had passed. None of it really made any sense to me. He and I, the best poker player in the history of the game were drinking wine and laughing together just a couple of days ago and now he's gone forever. I never understood what I did up to that point in my life that I was given the complete beauty of being able to spend that final moment with him. I think I cried for a couple of hours and my mother just left me alone. She knew how hard it must have been on me given the circumstances and I was still trying to put together all of the pieces. I felt awful. I felt like I should do something personally and initially towards his family and let them know about the moment we had together. I figured that they had enough feedback coming their way at this time that they didn't need to hear from a random kid about the death of their late loved one. He would have enough individuals to praise him over the course of the next few weeks. I had two choices. Either I head back to Vegas to go to his funeral out of respect, or I carry on what he told me to do. Go on the road and play tournaments. To learn what that kind of life is like. To see if it was something that I would take in for a more inspiring profession, or continue to enjoy the tension of high stakes cash games and degenerate fallout in the pits somewhere.

When I finally pulled myself together and took a shower, I saw that there was a tournament this weekend coming up with a tour in Indiana. About an hour drive from my house, but as close as a tour was going to get to Chicago any time soon. I laughed at the timing given how close the distance was, but it is what it is at this point. The main event was $2,500 and they were offering $500 satellites into the tournament all week. I figured that it would be best to go there and play one of these satellites, if not a few. I had never been to that casino even though it was just outside of the city limits. It would give me some tournament practice and also get me established for the week ahead of me. I was going to play the tournament either way. Whether I won the satellite or bought in right away, I was going to find a way to fulfill Chip's request.

I packed a bag for the week and headed to the casino that is next to it where all of us stayed for the weekends. It was just across the bay and literally a five minute drive from where the tournament was going to be. I was still emotionally and physically drained. I had random moments where I would tear up thinking that Chip wasn't around anymore. I don't think I would be like this if I didn't get a chance to spend the time with him that I did. It just all seemed so more intense and real to me since I was most likely the last player he ever played the game with. It was special to me and still is. But, I had to focus on the future and what was in front of me. Given my $50k win the last time I was in Vegas this past week, my bankroll shot back up to $700k. I was going to play this tournament either way, but I needed some tournament practice before I just dove in this weekend coming up. I decided to head over Wednesday to play a satellite and go from there.

I think there were 100 players or so in the satellite and the buy in was somewhere around $450. For anyone that doesn't understand what a satellite is, it's a chance to win your way into a tournament for a less amount of money. Easy way to explain it is if we were trying to win a seat into a $1,000 tournament and ten of us put up $100. We would play until one of us had all the chips and then that individual wins the seat. Or if we all put up $200, the top two would win a seat and so on. For a tournament such as this, with 100 players playing the satellite and a $450 buy in, my guess is $50 went to the house per buy-in and the remaining $400 was thrown into the prize pool multiplied by 100 players. Given that, there is $40k that goes towards the prize pool. If you divide that number by the total buy-in, which is $2,500 if I remember correctly, that comes out to exactly 16 seats were awarded that night through the satellite to the main event. And I made sure that I was going to be one of them.

When we were down to the final 17 players, I had the largest stack in the room, somewhere around

$125k. I busted out the last player when he went all in for $10k with AJ and I had pocket 6s. Nothing came from it and I had eliminated the final player and won the first satellite I had ever played as the chip leader. Granted being the chip leader didn't really matter because the remaining 16 players all received the same seat. I felt like it was Chip that was sitting on my shoulder that guided me through all of it. That was only the first stage though since the tournament wasn't for another two days. I trusted myself, but I wanted to keep on testing myself with practice. Even though I had won a seat Wednesday night, I decided to come back Thursday night as well and play the same tournament. If by chance I would win a seat again, I could sell it back to the casino for chips or cash and claim the value. I felt like I needed to do this because tournament poker is nothing like playing high stakes cash games. There are different procedures and thought processes that you need to take in with every decision that you make in order to be successful. I definitely needed to put myself into those situations as often as possible before Friday if I wanted to stand a chance. I came back again for round two and there were twice as many entrants since it was the day before the main event began.

Talk began to fly with my face being back in the area. People were accustomed and used to the stories they had been hearing about me out on the west coast and the nosebleed stakes I was playing, that they were confused as to why they were seeing me here in local casinos again. I had plenty of short conversations in the last two days with people stopping me on breaks or looking up when we were taking our seats and seeing me at the same table as them. I never brought up a word about Chip out of respect. I decided to tell them that I am going to try and travel for a while and give the tournament scene a shot. I felt that even after winning a seat the night before that I had already accomplished something. Tournaments are exhausting and filled with so much variance. It might look simplistic and a walk in the park when you see the final six players on television and everyone is so happy already, but getting to that moment is filled with a path of decisions and millions of land mines and intense tournament life survival decisions. It is extremely difficult to be a professional tournament player.

The boat that we played on, the poker room was on the top floor and it was the only poker room that I ever played in that had windows surrounding it. It faced out over Lake Michigan. I was playing the nightly satellite and as I watched the sunset go down that evening, I began to tear up. I was an emotional person back then. Everything that I was doing was so much more intense than that of a regular life of a 22 year old. Who should be in a dorm room or an apartment building studying for his finals or making bad decisions and begin pregaming in the afternoon instead. But I was here. Back in Chicago and doing something out of spite because of a guy that is now dead and I have to take his advice as far as I could. Alcohol wouldn't help, advice wouldn't help. Pretty much the only thing that would make me smile at the end of the day was winning. Winning everything, winning every fucking tournament that I ever came in contact with from here on out. All because of that sunset and those colors and the long island that was flowing down my throat. Because it was simply one of those moments in life where you didn't ignore what was staring you right in the face. This was the beauty of life that I had been searching for and it was right here beside me. I don't know until this day if Chip was standing over me, or if it was all just perfect timing. But I had never been more at peace with myself than I did right now.

I won another seat. I finished this time with close to $250k in tournament chips and was easily the leader by the time the final 31 of us had won the prize. I had finished both satellites as the chip leader and won seats on both nights. I sold my second seat back to the casino and pocketed the $2500 and walked to the door. Given the time and expectations, I came out as perfect player. It was early Friday morning by the time that we finished and we had a decision whether we wanted to play flights A, B or C. Flight A was going to be Friday night and Flights B and C were on Saturday. I decided to take flight C so that I could have some time to rest. For whatever reason I was quite exhausted from playing back to back days and over twenty hours of satellites. I definitely needed Friday off and decided to literally just lie in my hotel room all day long and watch television. I had a nice two hour long conversation with my father leading into it. I don't remember if I ever told him about Chip, but like I said before I was quite emotional as of lately. I had gotten a lot of recognition the last 48 hours being back in town and seeing faces I hadn't seen for quite some time. Seemed like if I wasn't in a hand, I was having a conversation with someone at the table about Vegas, a curious floor man or someone walking over from another table, it never seemed to end really. I got used to it, but at the same time I wanted to focus on what was going on around me too. So I was proud of myself that I got through those distractions, for now.

It felt good to just lie around in my room, order room service and have no worries for the next 48 hours. Which is definitely something that I wasn't used to having flowing through my conscious, I usually always wanted to gamble one way or the other. But I was more content and trying my best to just focus on this tournament ahead of me. The blogs on the internet were talking about Chip and people had been asking me if I had seen him at all leading up to his death and I just neglected. I knew that if I said yes then it would just lead into more conversations that I didn't want to be a part of. It was beyond special what Chip and I had and I wanted to keep it that way to the best of my ability.

My start time that Saturday afternoon was somewhere around 4pm I think and we were going to play until 10% of that field was remaining or until two in the morning. I grabbed a drink from the hotel bar where I was staying and grabbed a ride with a couple buddies of mine. My drink was finished by the time we got there and I grabbed another one from the second floor bar and finally walked upstairs to the tournament room. Flight B was finishing up and getting ready to end their day. It looked like there was going to be about 35 players left from that field with maybe 120 players or so that started that morning. I assumed that Friday night's turnout was similar, but didn't really care enough to ask. I had a number in my head that first place for this tournament would be somewhere between $200k & $250k. I got my seat assignment and made my way to my table.

I was doing horrific but somehow holding my ground. I was also trying to stay as sober as I could. I was sipping on maybe my fourth captain and coke since the tournament started a handful of hours ago, but feeling alright. Play became more strenuous and crucial as levels rose up. I was used to the action staying the same and me adjusting to the game as the feeling came to me in cash games. But with tournaments, as the levels continued to tack on and the clock keeps going forward, your stakes became higher and you need to learn how to adjust accordingly. That's where gambling finds its name. You needed to learn how to pick your spots, be conservative and at the drop of a dime you needed to know how to gamble. We all know I had that part checked off my list.

With thirty minutes left in the day and 45 of us remaining in the flight, I was down to $12k with the blinds at $1k/2k. Better known as six big blinds and as short stacked as you can almost get for a tournament. The next hand I would be under the gun and coming down to my last few chances before I had to make a move at making something happen. I was under the gun and the dealer dealt the first card and then the second. It was like a sign from Chip, I took a sip from my drink and I smiled, I had pocket aces. I thought for a few seconds and made myself aware of my surroundings and went all in. The guy to the left of me called, the button called as did both of the blinds. I love getting all of the action, but this gave me a greater chance of being knocked out too. In the length of my career I can honestly only count on my hand the few times I ever flopped aces full, but this was one of them. The flop panned out A88 and I was pretty much in the clear to have a stack of $60k+. It went checks around all the way to the river and I flipped over my hand in silence. The entire table mucked and a buddy of mine from the rail clapped his hands a few times. The very next hand I was in the big blind and it was folded around to the button, he shipped it with pocket 9s just to have me look down at pocket jacks. I snapped called the $15k and won that pot too. So in just two hands I went from $12k to $75k. I was comfortable again, but still had plenty of more work to do.

The day ended about twenty minutes later and I was content on my stack size. It sounded like between the three flights that would all return Sunday afternoon for a compounded day two, there would be about 85 of us remaining. First place was $225k and the top 34 players would receive at least $3200. I ordered a double of something after my couple of victories and it gave me a good buzz going into the night. We would come back tomorrow at 2pm to play down to the final six and the T.V. table. We bagged up our chips and headed back to the hotel. I made it back to my room and hit my pillow with a smile on my face.

The following morning we woke up around noon and met downstairs for lunch. We still had about an hour until the day started. Two of my other friends were still in with healthy stack sizes too. That was one of the most fascinating times as a poker professional, going deep into a tournament of that magnitude with close friends. It created a deeper bond between all of you. That would then bounce back in the tournament or later on when you're traveling on the road together when you just need some positive feedback. You were brothers.

We made our way over and up to the poker room. We finally got to see who survived the first couple of flights before ours and there were plenty of familiar faces. We engaged in some conversation here and there and then gave each other our good luck wishes and found our seats. I ran to the bar really quick and grabbed a drink since the waitresses there took forever. I was so used to Vegas type service I guess.

This day in general took forever. I was playing decent, but still didn't really know what I was doing. Tournament poker was a whole different game. All of these players were obsessed with the first place prize being this close that they tensed up and stopped gambling as much. Given that, I was able to mess with them a little bit and be aggressive. I guess you can say that I played as aggressive as I could leading up to the money burst, then I slowed down after. When the bubble broke, I had about $300k and I think the blinds were $6k/$12k. I was sitting alright for now.

We made it down to the final table and we were guaranteed somewhere around $25k. It was nice cash, but first place was ten times that amount and meant way more to me because of Chip. It took almost three hours to bust out the next three players and before I knew it we were down to the final six players, guaranteed $40k and I was going to be on national television. It was an accomplishment all in itself for me. I was proud of myself. I missed the guy, but in a sense I was doing all of this for him and it was as if I was just tagging along for the ride and he was in the driver's seat. We bagged up our chips one more time and had to be back at ten in the morning for interviews and get prepped.

I didn't sleep a wink. I just kind of stared out my hotel room and was paralyzed. My longtime friends and family had never seen me play a hand of poker. Now they were going to get a chance to see me play on national television and at a shot of $225k. It's a lot of money to anyone unless you're dead. Another drink was poured and six in the morning rolled around. There was that sunrise that I had seen so many times in the last couple of years. Then another drink was poured and it was seven in the morning. Before I knew it I was taking a shower with a drink resting on the toilet head. I had a buddy of mine drive me over to the casino for the interviews and I tried to pull myself together. I was incredibly intoxicated and on zero sleep. Not exactly the best condition you wanted to be in for your first appearance on national television.

They had shut down the poker room except for a handful of tables and turned it completely into a studio. I pounded two waters and a steak and eggs before it was my turn for my interview and I think I was alright. Mixed in with ten sprays of cologne, I was in for the clear. They asked me standard questions since my profession was what it was and I was who I was. I wasn't too used to giving interviews really. But the country was going to see this and I just answered their questions as they came to me. I don't really remember any of it, not because of the alcohol but just because of the element. There I was giving an interview for a national television production for poker. Did this mean that I finally made it? Who knew really, I don't even know to this day. This was just a moment that I was going to be given full capability of winning a tournament that I never would have played in if it wasn't for Chip and the advice that he gave me just a week before. The drawn out emotions I had and the desire I held inside of me to make this more of a reality, was my motivation for his memory.

An hour later I would be the first to bust out in 6th place and on just the third hand of play. I called a raise preflop with AQ instead of being aggressive with it and either re-raising or going all in. Unfortunately the flop came up A86, I checked and my opponent bet $100k, I went all in for about $550k and he snap called, tabeling A6 for two pair. Nothing panned out for me and I made my way to the back exit and to the deck of the boat looking out onto the lake. I didn't cry, but I just stood out there for as long as I could. Until one of the tour's hosts came and found me because I still had to give my post final table interview. I was unaware this was something I had to do, but I had to follow through the process in order to get paid. She was a smoking hot host too, which made the moment a little less annoying.

When I got cashed out, they only kept $20k in the cage and I guess they expected all of us to get paid out with checks or bank wires. Being the asshole that I am and as upset as I was, I asked to be paid out in cash. A complete inconvenience because security had to go down to the vault to pick up the $40k and come back to the cage. I just wanted to head back to Vegas and on with my life at this point. I can't recall one cash session prior to that where I felt this sad with myself. Not even an ounce of frustration, but I was literally just extremely sad and felt like a part of me had been ripped out. Did I succeed because I got this far in my first major tournament? Or did I fail because I didn't win the entire thing? The answer can go both ways the more I thought about it. But then I thought about what Chip said. That poker isn't about one day or two days, it's about every day. Every day is important for a poker player. The swings can be devastating, but consistently winning will keep you alive and on towards a successful path. When I remembered those words from him, all of a sudden I was alright. I pocketed the $40k, tipped the ladies at the cage $500 for their time and made my way to the exit with three security guards, shaking all of the floor men's hands on the way out. Departing with an entourage of about fifteen guys that came to support me. This was a good experience. Today was a good day.

When I left, I packed up my shit at the hotel and went home to see my mom and to drop off some cash for her. When I walked in, I lost it. I put the $40k down on the computer table and released a tremendous amount of tears and emotion on top of the stack of money. I think they were happy tears though. I honestly couldn't believe the scenario I just put myself through given the circumstances and I came out as a winner. My bankroll was shadowing around $750k and I needed to head back to Vegas. I left $20k at home and took the other $20k and headed to the airport. Life goes on.

The rest of the year was alright. I won another $60k in the next few weeks in cash games. Given expenses and everything, going into 2008 my bankroll was somewhere around $800k. I had won a seat into Bellagio's $15k main event but came up short missing out on $2 million for first place. But it had been one hell of a year. It was a year that I obviously can still remember bits and pieces of, but I'm still missing out on a lot of days and hours and moments. I've basically just accepted the fact that those days are gone forever. I wasn't ready to leave 2007, but I knew that my future was anxiously waiting in 2008. So I tipped my hat to the previous 365 days and raised my glass to the year to come.

I kicked it off early with getting stuck in a snow storm on my way back from U of I on the first day of the year. Mindy was going to Hawaii the following day for a couple of weeks and she had to be back on the first. I don't think we went more than twenty miles per hour the entire trip back. So it was quite the introduction to the brand new year. I was ready to get out of Chicago. The last two weeks that I was in town for the holidays may have been the longest amount of time that I had spent in Illinois in almost four years. So I missed the airport and traveling.

Over the course of the next four months I would go on an absolute terror. Something that a lot of people had never seen before and I began to become recognizable all over the country. Television, magazines, or just word of mouth, it seemed like anywhere I went I was the talk of the room when I walked in. Players would leave their tables just to come watch me play a few hands. Or if I was out in the pits, people would crowd around my table and watch me gamble. I started traveling to tours on the east coast and the west coast. I was cashing in regular tournaments and earning player of the year points, but I was absolutely dominating the nightly tournaments. Each tour has a set of nightly tournaments that the players can jump into if they busted out of the daily prelim tournament. They ranged anywhere from $220 to $1,100. From the beginning of the year until the end of April, I played in 58 of them, cashed in 39 of them, won 17 of them and won more than $650k. Granted, also over that time period my blackjack addiction had become an awful demoralization. I had dropped back probably $600k of that. But still, my reputation was growing entirely and I was happy with being called the best up and coming gambler in the country. I lost that title of being the best poker player in Chicago since I had become a degenerate gambler. I was betting sports, backing players, playing blackjack for 48 hours straight, playing the highest stakes in the world and finally became a chronic alcoholic. I was spending more time binging and in the pits, than focusing on poker. But in the midst of it all, I was still winning almost 28% of the tournaments I was playing. A number that is still mind boggling given the fact that a good tournament player should only cash in just 15% of his tournaments, and maybe win less than 1% of them, I was flat out winning more than some entire field's stats combined.

But I was traveling. I wasn't just taking the normal flights from Chicago to Vegas anymore. I went to New Orleans, Atlantic City, Omaha, L.A., Reno, San Jose, Foxwoods, Tunica, Shakopee and Biloxi. I pretty much won a tournament in every city. There were articles being written about me comparing me to the late Stu Ungar and his phenomenal talent for gambling while mixed in with his cocaine addiction as to mine with alcohol. How we appeared to be a mirror image of each other. Midwestern States magazine actually wrote an article about me and him including our similarities. How we would be the ultimate heads up match of the century based off of our sickness for the game and addiction with our own selective poisons. How we were math wizards and never lost playing gin for substantial amounts of money. I was winning everything and was intoxicated through all of it. The only time I was sober were the times that I was sleeping, if I was lucky. Honestly I was afraid that if I slowed down and sobered up that I would stop winning since it seemed to be some type of an ingredient to my success. That thought in an entirety of not being successful and being scared of my future was exhausting. So I pretty much didn't stop drinking for a single minute for the rest of my career.

My first episode of the tournament I got 6th place in finally aired on television. My friends and family were blowing up my phones and social media alike. I would be out at random bars and I would look up and see myself on the T.V. Catching everyone's attention and I would always be surrounded with questions, people buying me drinks and girls. The local bars that we would go out at in the summertime when everyone was home from college were packed every night since all of us had just now started turning of legal age. It was a simple hangout and always became a high school reunion. It became widely known of my success and what I was doing. There were times that we had to leave bars because of the attention I was getting and it was taking away from spending time with my friends and Mindy. It wasn't unlikely for me to run up $400 tabs and tipping enormous amounts along with it. Which took notice on the waitresses and sometimes they would argue on who got the chance to serve me and my friends on certain nights. I felt famous. Between the attention I got back home from local people and being noticed at every tournament stop I was going on, it all finally clicked to me. Sometimes though, it was frustrating and became quite the nuisance when you see how non-caring the human behavior can reach sometimes. Some people were just straight rude and not aware of their surroundings in some situations. But you had to learn to take the good with bad and understand that life isn't all love and roses.

The tour returned to Indiana in April, the same tour that was here four months prior that I whiffed and got 6th place in. The buy-in was smaller, only $2200 this time. I was one of the hottest players on the circuit, both in nightly tournaments and high stakes cash games. I had one thing on my mind when I came back to Chicago, I was going to win this thing. I had gained so much momentum from traveling all over the country these last few months. I felt like I was a new player with more knowledge and maturity under my belt for the game and life in general. What a better time than now to bring it on home and do it for my boys and my family. I flew back to Chicago the day of the tournament, so I didn't have any time to play any satellites. The only reason I was playing satellites before that first time was to practice and get into a groove. I felt like I didn't need that anymore given my recent success and results.

I walked into the room and it was the normal feeling of people looking at me and letting others know I had arrived. The registration was in the back and there wasn't really an aisle to get there. You sort of just had to weave your way through the tables. I heard people calling out my name and saw a few guys I knew that wanted me to shake their hands and talk. I kept giving them the give me a minute signal so I could get my registration in and get my seat assignment. I was always up for talking to people when I was home in Chicago. It was all poker talk in the end. We could bring up hands that we played together or discussed months ago and would still remember certain details. Poker players, the good ones at least, established a memory that impressed me all the time. And anyone that plays cards can agree with me on that. You may not see someone for months and the second you see them you may instantly go back to that last time you played against them and remember a certain scenario. It always impressed me. Except when I had no clue what they were talking about!

I finished my flight with $117k and somewhere in the top 5 for the day and probably top 10 between the three flights combined. There were 311 entrants, top 31 made $3200 and first place was $180k. I returned to day two sober for once. I drank a lot on day one, but I don't contribute that to my stack size. Everything just kind of went right. My AK was beating pocket pairs all in pre-flop, I was hitting flushes on the turn and not sweating them all the way until the river. I was three betting and four betting guys trying to bluff me. I was just playing all around great poker, but I still had a long ways to go to win that title.

We came back to day two and I started the day off with a seven and seven. It was probably one of my favorite laid back drinks that just went down like water and always gave me a nice buzz. The day went back as expected and it seemed like every time I pulled out my blackberry, I had fifteen new text messages from my buddies asking me for updates.

Keep in mind this is way before intense social media. So it wasn't as easy to set up mass updates to everyone. When I think about it then compared to now, it's an exhausting comparison. I was a constant texting machine, still am and my phone charger was always in my pocket. I was regularly updating people on the outside world as to how I was doing.

When we made it down to the final seven players, I had about $500k and the blinds were huge, but I was holding my own. I had to make back to back final T.V. tables. There was no way I was going to get this close on the T.V. bubble and not make it. I raised double the big blind with pocket jacks and the big blind immediately went all in. The chances of him having a hand better than mine when we were seven handed was extremely slim. I was actually hoping that he was three bet shipping with pocket eights through pocket tens and I had him dominated. On the other hand, I was absolutely more than willing to lose my chips knowing I made the right call if he had AQ or AK and he discovered a pair along the way to knock me out. It was in the early hours of the morning, I was drunk and guaranteed $21k, fuck it. I called and he flipped over pocket kings. One of the three hands I undeniably didn't want to see. We had to wait like two minutes for cameras to get in place and what not which was so prolonging I wanted to snap. I had to stare at his hand that had me just crushed. But it was moments like this where you just trusted your gut instinct and knew it was the right call. Whether he had you beat or not, there's still a million ways these cards could pan out that I could more than double up my stack. The dealer panned it out.

JJQ. I flopped quads.

Yes! I screamed louder than I could explain through words if I wanted to. Just to add insult to injury he rivered a king for kings full which was useless by that point. I doubled up and was sitting on upwards of $1 million and sitting pretty.

Just by an act of God, I was in the big blind the next hand and the player under the gun openly shipped it for $900k with A7 trying to steal the blinds and antes. I looked down just to find pocket aces! I snap called and he had about 1.1 million, so this was for our tournament lives pretty much. The board panned out nothing for him and just like that I had a little bit over $2 million and he was crushed down to less than $100k. A few hands later we busted the final player and we made the final six. It was actually the first time in the history of the tour that the same person had made back to back final T.V. tables at the same location. So that was exciting. I was the chip leader with $2.1 million, the next closest player had $1 million less than me and players third through six were in ranges of $125k-$400k. So I had the remaining players absolutely dominated in chip stacks.

At least this time when I went back home to my mother's, I was able to sleep for a few hours. I called my father on the ride home and I told him the good news that I made the final table again. He had work the following day, but I practically begged him and told him that he had to come see me play. He had never seen me play poker before, ever. He even missed the first time I was on T.V. too. But he never missed anything that meant everything to me. I was destined, determined and completely convinced that I was going to win this tournament. He said he would be at my house early and ride along with me for the hour long journey back to the casino and I couldn't have been happier that he was going to be there with me. Only because of the arguments we had gotten into in the beginning of my career with his disagreements on my future decisions. This was definitely important to me for him to see this finally. What a better spotlight to be under.

He showed up early since I had to be back there early for interviews just like before. It was raining out that day and it still upsets me that I can't remember any of the conversation we had on the way to the tournament. I treasured all of those moments that I had with my father. I didn't know anyone in my life at 22 years old that they could call their parents their best friends. I remember that my phone was blowing up constantly with texts and phone calls and people wishing me the best of luck. It makes me sad now that I remember the kind of support I had for my career back then. Now it's just walking in a deserted area somewhere and nonexistent to some extent.

We arrived, I checked in, grabbed a drink and I was first up to do my interviews since I was the chip leader. When I was finished it was about eleven in the morning and we had about an hour until we started playing. My friends showed up which became an immediate drinking festivity.

They were all extremely happy for me since all of them were convinced that I was going to win this thing and pocket the $180k first place prize. Probably pick up the tab that night in a celebration dinner worth more than $1,500. About ten of my closest poker friends showed up and we all took shots before I even started playing. I grabbed another captain and coke towards the end of the hour and they made the announcement for us to take our seats. I sat in seat two and they did player introductions. The place went nuts when my name was called. I was calm, relaxed and according to the magazines and everyone else I knew, I was the hottest player in the country right now. There's no reason why I shouldn't win this tournament.

I finished third. The alcohol caught up to me mixed in with some bad plays and I walked to the same cage and saw the same cashier ladies with a disappointed prize of $54k. I was pissed. The only thing that I was happy about was that about fifteen minutes into play I looked over and saw Mindy. She had literally been excused from one of her college final exams because her professor enjoyed the game of poker, drove up from U of I and surprised me. She was perfect and that's a moment I will never forget. My father and my girlfriend mixed in with the thought of my mother were the ultimate motivation for me to win that fucking tournament. But I failed. I was also upset with myself on the assuming thought that I was going to win $180k that day, that I didn't bring some type of a backpack or anything to carry the cash. My dad stashed $20k in his pockets and I threw the other $35k in mine and we strolled on out of there at our own pace with two bodyguards.

I was upset. He was upset. He wanted me to win. I understood. I was used to losing and winning sessions almost three and four times these magnitudes that didn't bother me. This one definitely bothered me because it was right there in front of me at my fingertips in front of the people that meant the most to me. To this day I wonder what that celebration would have been like had I won. What we would have done that night or the weeks going forward. It's really too many what ifs at this point to try and think about.

I wanted nothing to do with the world. I just wanted to be with Mindy. She came all the way up here to surprise me so of course I was going to take the ride back with her to U of I. And I did. My father and I drove in the same car back to my mother's house and she followed. I dropped off $50k to my safe at my house, threw $5k in my pocket and we continued on our way to U of I.

That very day pretty much put a cease to my tournament career. It was never the same for me after that. I simply couldn't recuperate from it. Just mentally the drive I had to make hotel arrangements and travel to cities I had never been to just wasn't of interest to me anymore. I was too upset that I blew what could have been the most amazing moment of my poker career. To win a tournament of that size in front of the people that meant the most to me. To pump your fist and turn around and hug your father and your friends, but I ruined it. Not because it was on national television again or the $180k first place prize, but because I had all of the right people there with me in that moment of time. I completely fucking blew it. My sexiness and determination for tournaments was completely murdered. I played a couple more going forward, but it just wasn't the same for me after that day. Magazines wrote articles about my disappearance from the nightly tournaments and just the tournament scene in general. Actually a fun fact, I had killed it so much in just the first four months of the year, I finished in first place for 2008 for nightly tournaments throughout the country. Even with me not playing for the last eight months of the year, I still conquered the title.

I still get upset that I didn't truly appreciate any of anything you just read in this chapter. I was so used to the high life I was living, the whiskey that naturally traveled with me and the money that I had, to really survive a more balanced poker lifestyle. My tournament days were over. My perfect girlfriend and I went back to U of I because I just needed time away from absolutely everything. The last four months of traveling all over the country and winning in ways I never expected, were inside of me now. I respected my game and was proud of myself if anything. I definitely missed the high stakes action and presidential suites. I think it was time to go back to my old ways and let my tournament career die on its own.

When we drove the two hours back to U of I and finally reached our destination back to her apartment, I woke up from sleeping the entire way.

"Who's Chip?" Mindy asked me.

"Why?"

"While you were sleeping you said, I wish Chip was here to see all of this."

To this day I still miss him. Because of his educated advice, I spent a few months on the road experiencing poker in ways I never would have thought of. A way that he thought would be acceptable and tolerable for me. That's just how good he was. He could just see inside of you. I got to see the country and mature in ways that I wouldn't had I kept up my same routine from going to Vegas from Chicago over and over again. I won over $800k playing tournament poker in those four months. But like I said I also lost back about $600k playing blackjack and betting sports. Which is ok, it was part of the profession and I had established that agreement years prior in advance with myself. Losing was sometimes the only learning experience. You needed to learn how to lose and establish ways to deal with it if you wanted to be successful with a gambling career.

In the end, I won over 20 tournaments in four months. I cashed in 60% of the tournaments I played in and did all of it highly intoxicated. But I was ready to go back to my degenerate ways in Vegas because that's just who I was and who I had become. I wished it was different and that I could stay on the path I was, but I just couldn't. I was too upset that I blew that one tournament the way I did in front of the people that meant the world to me.

I spent an amazing week at U of I with Mindy. My bankroll was somewhere around $875k and it was finally that time I became a millionaire. I made a phone call to O'Hare Airport for a private jet to Vegas.

It was time to change things up and make my next dream a reality.

"If I could sell my experiences and stories for what they have cost me, I'd have money forever."

Pinnacle-

When I showed up at O'Hare to head back to Vegas, mistakenly they had sent my flight crew to Midway on accident. Nicely, they threw me in a helicopter and we took the short ride to the other airport in Chicago where my jet was. The private jet was just exquisite and kind of overwhelming. I had never taken one before and figured I should spend my winnings on something other than alcohol, gambling and my friends for a change. They always say that you should spend a certain amount of your check on yourself so that you can appreciate what it is that you're doing for a living. I didn't exactly receive a check, but I did appreciate the things that I did with my money. I just didn't appreciate the cash or know the value of any of it compared to the real world. I bought cars, watches and everything else that made other people happy.

They were going to charge me $1.25 per mile, plus other expenses. All in all it came out to about $2800 for a one way trip to Vegas from Chicago for just me on a 7 passenger private jet. My stewardess was absolutely gorgeous and she actually sat with me for the majority of the flight since I was the only passenger. She went to school in Texas, was rather short and had long dark hair. I am not positive if there is anything sexier than a girl with a southern accent either. She was in her mid-twenties and wanted to be a stewardess her whole life apparently. Her uncle was one of the owners of the company, so it worked out for her. I told her all about my Vegas life and surprisingly enough she was a fan of poker, so she had plenty of questions. She got me good and drunk too. I finished almost two bottles of merlot by the time we landed. It was nice to sit there and have a friend for a few hours to talk to. I honestly would have probably just fell asleep for the majority of the flight and not been able to enjoy my expensive purchase.

It felt good to be back in Vegas. It was the first time in my career I think where I actually missed this town. I had spent the last ten days in Champaign after getting third place in that last tournament. I just needed time away from everything. I wanted to spend time with my friends that I hadn't seen in quite a while and of course time with Mindy. I had been on the go for literally almost five months straight. I was living in and out of airports and hotel rooms, spending long hours gambling and trying to breathe in between if I had a chance. Sure it sounds like it was the same lifestyle from before, but tournament life is the exact opposite of a degenerate gambler's life. Plus like I said, I became a noticeable player all over the country. I was constantly either giving an interview or having a conversation with someone about my career. That can ultimately be exhausting and time consuming if you aren't ready for it.

I had a limo waiting for me off the runway when we pulled into the hanger and I couldn't wait to get back to the Bellagio and up to my suite. I missed the smells of the hotel's carpets that had just been cleaned. Or the fact that everyone was always happy and that all of the women were always beautiful and dressed to impress. Or maybe it was the constant playing of 90s music and hits from today on the loud speakers. It was home to me. We pulled up to the circle driveway and I tipped the driver $50 and made my way into the lobby. The glass flowers above that dressed the ceiling were right where I left them. Along with Arthur the gentleman always playing the piano at the corner cigar bar, dressed in his usual tuxedo. I checked in and made my way upstairs. A path that I had missed walking a few times a week that had recently been cut down to just three times over the course of the last five months. Nothing had changed, but everything seemed to feel different.

The suite was gorgeous as always. It was my own little mansion, minus the ghosts and butlers of course. They put the couch by the window as requested and my energy drinks were nestled nicely in a bucket with ice. The suite was a little larger than the ones I had stayed in before. Maybe since they saw that I hadn't been around for a while, they wanted to capture my attention just a little bit more. You never know with these people. I could never and will ever not take their hospitality for granted. Bellagio did nothing but treat me right and it made my poker career that much more memorable for the rest of my life. Sure I stayed at other hotels all over the strip and the country, but I will always come back to Bellagio and their staff and how they treat their customers. All class acts and that's why it's a five star hotel.

I really didn't know what to do with myself now. It had been such a long time since I had been back without the purpose of playing a tournament that I sort of forgot what it was like to just have the urge to want to be a degenerate and gamble at anything. Since I already drank two bottles of wine on the jet, I opened up my bar and found another bottle of merlot and cracked it open and poured myself a glass. Wine can be just as dangerous as anything else. If I started drinking wine, I couldn't start mixing it with other alcohol, I had to stay with it. I figured that I should probably find some dinner and I would go from there. I didn't know what I had a taste for, so I decided to walk downstairs and see what I could find.

I stopped at one of the cages and picked up $100k from my security box. I threw $5k on a baseball game to start my gambling fix off and grabbed dinner in the meantime. I hadn't eaten since lunch really and all the wine kind of drowned me out. I enjoyed a fascinating 14oz steak and all the vegetables in the world. It was just what I needed.

Only annoying part about going to dinner at nice restaurants in Vegas when you're alone is the fact that everyone there is with people they love or in large groups. As I stated before, to divert from having to wait in long lines for a table, I would just sit at the bar and blend in that way.

Bellagio was quiet for once and I figured I would get my degeneracy back up and running with some blackjack. I made my way over to the high limit pits and was greeted by the floor manager Mikey who I hadn't seen in almost three months. He gave me the handshake and half hug thing and it was good to see him. He was a great guy. He had been working in Vegas for over thirty years and had four daughters. An honest working gentleman that I don't think had ever told me no to anything I ever wanted. One time for whatever reason I had a dying taste for a Big Mac from McDonald's and he made one of his dealers run there on her break to get me one. In a year and a half he was probably by far my most favorite floor man in the country.

I bought in for $25k and asked the waitress for another merlot. The dealer gave me $5k in $500 chips and the remaining $20k in $1k chips. I threw my feet up on the chair next to me and got to work. It felt good to be staring down at chips again with actual money value on them. The way they sounded and how easy they were to be stacked was just the sexiest thing a degenerate could ask for. See with tournaments, you give the cage your buy-in for the tournament and it could be hours or even days, if you make the money that is, to get paid out on your winnings. Obviously with cash games or out in the pits, it's all right there in front of you constantly. You're watching the cash be thrown around and taken from you or paid to you in just a few seconds all the time.

I started out betting $500-$1,500 a hand for the first couple of hours. I had a few hands where I had a spread of three or four hands across the board and won them. I had a double down for $15k that I lost in an ugly way when splitting two 9s against the dealer's 3. I made two 19s but she panned out a 20 somehow.

Six hours had come and gone and I was up about $35k. I was dead exhausted and decided to call it a night. I tipped Mikey $100 and promised him that he will be seeing more of me in the days to come.

I ended up losing my baseball bet that I made earlier in the night for $5k, so I was up $30k on the day. I didn't even want to know how much wine I had in me at this point, but I needed some type of greasy burger and fried something to put in my stomach or I was going to wake up feeling awful. I headed back to my room and ordered $50 worth of room service. En route was a huge burger with a salad and hot fudge dripped onto mint chocolate chip ice cream. Hell yes!

To this day I am still obsessed with food. Part of me blames it on having access to such delicious dishes for over four years, especially since everything at Bellagio was free for me. It always surprised me that I was never more than maybe 140 pounds back then. I was eating exquisite meals all the time. My only guesses were the consumption of alcohol and the fact that I sometimes would only have one meal a day if any.

I poured myself another glass of wine and lied down on the couch that was rested next to the cathedral high windows and watched Vegas as it moved on past my window. While waiting for the room service to arrive, I stared at the moon through my feet that were up against the window and smiled. What an emotional ride the last five months had been. From traveling constantly to different destinations other than Vegas, I had acquired a slim dip of maturity and professionalism. I started to become nicer to people and was falling more in love with Mindy since I was doing things out of my ordinary routine. Chip gave me a chance to see life through a different kind of view. It inspired me more for my future in the game and how important having a family one day meant to me and that was essential. Room service arrived and I turned on some music and pigged out. I was going to sleep good tonight.

I woke up the following afternoon around three. I desperately needed a hot shower. One of those hot showers where you just sit there for like an hour and soak it all in and let the alcohol find its way out. I was surprised that I didn't have a hangover at all, which is always a plus. Maybe it was the late night room service or the fact that I had just slept for about ten hours. But shit, I have had hangovers so bad where I had to sit on the floor of the shower because I couldn't even stand up. I'm sure I had one hell of a time the night before, but no one enjoys a brutal hangover. I cracked a beer and took an hour long shower.

I didn't really know what my plans were for the day. I missed playing poker and when I walked past the poker room last night to make that sports bet, I saw that there was a few high stakes games going. It was probably best that I play some cash to get my foot back in the door with that world again. It was hot as fuck out. Being the middle of May it was somewhere around 100 degrees and I didn't feel like walking to another casino to find lunch. There was a little deli place next to the sports book called "Snacks" and they had the most fabulous BLT and clam chowder a man could ever ask for. It became my choice of meal for the day and I made my way over to the poker room to see what kind of action was going on. Surprisingly enough there was a lot. Almost all of the tables were filled and four of the five high stakes games were going. The highest was $400/$800 limit hold-em only, $100/$200 and the other two were the regular $10/$20 NL games that ran around the clock. The $400/$800 game was four handed and looked sexy as ever. I put $10k on a baseball game so I could sweat some action on the televisions that hung above our heads when I wasn't in a hand. I gave the floor man $100k to buy-in with in the cash game just to be obnoxious. He ran over to the cage and got my chips for me. It had been such a long time since I sat and played cash games that I wanted some ammo in front of me for comfort. Any other day of the week a normal buy-in for that game is about $20k. He came back with $50k in $500s, $30k in $1ks and $20k in $100s.

I knew two of the four players. One of them was a well-known pro and the other was a high stakes player from California. These guys migrated all over the west coast wherever the biggest games were. I asked why he was in town and he said that there was supposed to be some other high stakes players showing up in the next few days to get stakes off that were higher than this. I threw him my number and told him to let me know if that's the case and you got yourself another player. I was dying to play higher, but I should still take my time and try to focus on this session right now. I ordered a jack and coke and got comfortable.

Action was absolutely chaotic. Every hand seemed to have a pot of $20k. The two gentlemen I didn't know, one was an Asian businessman from Hong Kong apparently and the other was an Italian stud that owned his own chain of restaurants out on the east coast somewhere. They were full of some gamble. I had been getting myself involved in a few pots here and there and I was worried that maybe I was playing too high stakes this early on. I hadn't played anything higher than $40/$80 in over five months. But with my confidence I had in myself and a small win the night before playing blackjack, I had no fear sitting down at this level. Short-handed games were my specialty and I needed to uphold that talent for myself. It was hard to find a full table of stakes this high. Usually it would just be a few players at a time willing to put a game together of this magnitude. You needed to know how to play short-handed in order to be successful at the nosebleed stakes.

I got caught up in a nice hand about an hour into play. I was already up $15k and I opted to two bet to $800 with K2ss, which means I am suited in spades in case you forgot. The button three bet me to $1200 and the big blind over called. I called behind and we saw a flop of Kxx one spade. The big blind checked to me and I bet $400, the guy to my right two bet me to $800 and the big blind folded. I called and the turn was another spade giving me a flush draw. I bet out $800 and got raised again to $1600. I figured he either had AA, AK or KQ. I was in the gambling mood and had a 24% chance of either rivering two pair or hitting my flush, so I made it $2400 to go and he came back with a raise to $3200. I called and the river was an offset 2 giving me two pair and I bet out $800. He just called and I flipped over my two pair quietly, he mucked and I scooped the $13k pot. Tipped the dealer $25 and was up around $23k.

I got up to stretch my legs and headed to the bathroom for a short break. When I came back to the table, there was only one player remaining and I asked where everyone had gone. I was only gone maybe five minutes. He said a few other players showed up and Bobby's Room was going to get a larger game off. I couldn't help myself, so I went to find out the details. I rounded the corner and there were the best of the best. I am sure most of you can think of a few names instantly and that's who was there. Mixed in with the players we already had, we had a full game almost. I walked in and asked what they were deciding on playing.

"Probably $1k/$2k ten game mix with $200/$400 PLO and NL games."

Well, I was in a gambling mood and all, but fuck. These stakes I could lose $200k in one hand if I wasn't careful enough. But if there was ever a time to do this it was now. My bankroll was around $900k and I was at the Pinnacle of my career. It was time.

"I'm in."

I walked back out to the cage by the pit where I had most of my cash buried. I grabbed another $300k from my safety box. I still had about $125k sitting on the table from the game I was playing in. I figured I would buy in for $200k and leave the rest in my pocket if I needed to reload. Praying to God that I wouldn't have to of course, but you just never know what can happen. I heard a quote once that you never know what kind of a poker player you are until you play at stakes you can't afford. It changes your game up to make better decisions and if you do it correctly, it can be a learning experience to better your career.

I bought in for $225k and put the other eight $25k chips in my pocket, hoping that's where they would stay. Just like that I was playing in the cathedral of poker rooms with the elite of the elite in the highest stake game the world had to offer.

I lost my first hand in Omaha Eight or Better. I was dealt A224 on a 35J flop. It was three bet before the flop and checked to me on the flop. I bet, keep in mind this is limit, I bet out $1k and got raised to $2k. The button over called and I decided to three bet to $3k. It was a huge flop for my hand. Any low card gave me the nut low and three cards gave me the wheel too. I was four betted to $4k and I decided to cap it at $5k. Both players called and we saw a turn of a Q. I bricked all of my outs, but thankfully still had one more card to come and I picked up a back door 4 high flush draw if need be. The big blind checked and I decided to bet $2k, the player to my left just called as did the big blind. The river was a king, so I missed my nut nut low draw but I hit a very small flush. Unfortunately, the big blind bet out and I was almost certain that he had a hand like A4xx with the nut flush. I called with the small flush and the world's best player on my left folded his hand. I was right and the big blind flipped up A497 with the nut flush and scooped the $30kish pot.

The hand that finally got me going in the right direction was an insane PLO hand. I was dealt AQJ9 with the AQdd and J9ss, it was potted before the flop and five of us saw the flop with $7,500 in the middle. The flop came down T87 with the T7dd. So I flopped the nut straight with the nut flush draw. The opening player potted it for $7,500, the player to my right called and I re-potted it to about $35k. The original player that bet out raised all in for $90k or so and I snap called assuming we had the same hand and I was just praying that diamonds would come for my flush so I could scoop it. Surprisingly enough he didn't have J9, he had KQ96 with the king high flush draw and lower straight. So I actually had him destroyed unless he somehow hits a higher straight than mine. But the turn was a 3 and the river was a 4 and I scooped the $200k pot. Just like that I was comfortable and already up about $110k. If I did my calculations correctly, that pot put me over a million dollar bankroll. I did it!

About six hours went by and a few guys had dropped out, but we were still four handed with almost $2 million on the table between all of us. We upped the limits to $1500/$3k for the limit games and $300/$600 for the NL and PLO games. It didn't look like any of us were going anywhere any time soon either. I was taking my time with the drinking because of the nosebleed stakes we were playing, but I still couldn't help myself really and was probably on my tenth jack and coke. Everyone was drinking though. The two Phil's ordered a bottle of Dom and the other player had been drinking scotch on the rocks since we started. There were a few smoking hot girls sitting around the table too, but I of course was alone. I almost wanted to call back that hooker company that screwed me over and have them send me a girl to the poker room immediately. But I of course didn't. I had about $550k in front of me and was cruising along.

I was impressed that these guys knew who I was since they stuck to the highest stakes and the largest buy-in tournaments the world had to offer. I was obviously doing alright in my career sticking to the lower amounts. We engaged in conversation the entire time that we were playing and told stories about traveling and what it was like behind the scenes of this lifestyle that we shared. We talked about hand secrets and discussed several theories for different plays in a variety games. Part of me drifted off though. I just realized that the last time I was in this room was that last night I had with Chip. I wanted to tell them that story, but I didn't want to bring it up either for plenty of reasons. Until now I have really held it to myself in regards to how inspiring that moment was to me. These guys were just normal guys, just like anyone else. They were just successful icons to the entire poker world.

Another six hours went by and we all ordered dinner to be sent to the table. I had an 18oz steak with some shrimp and soup. I don't remember what they ordered. But the action was still flowing and we had another well-known player sit down and join us. We were five handed now. We took out a few of the games at this point and we were only playing limit hold-em, Stud Eight or Better, PLO,

NL and 2-7 Triple Draw. But the stakes stayed the same.

I made a hero call in this NL hand. I felt like the way Phil played it was just not like him at all. I was dealt J8hh in NL and made it $2200 to go, Phil made it $7400 and I called. The flop came down 822 and I checked. He bet out $11.2k and I opted to raise it to $23k. He came back with two $25k chips making it $50k straight to go. I called and the turn was a 3. I decided to check and he fired out $45k. He hadn't been this aggressive at all surprisingly all session in the NL portion. He was making small bets along the way for value and the only hand I can recall him betting like this was a hand where he missed a flush draw and was aggressive the whole way. But I did have a couple things I was worried about on the river if I called this $45k bet on the turn. Even though I put him on just AK, I am still going to be paranoid about any high card that comes out over an 8. Literally the only river I am happy with is another 8. And I felt like he was going to bet huge since the pot is going to be in the $200k range. He's going to fire at least $100k on the river I felt if not more. But I called the $45k on the turn and prayed. The river was another 2 and the final board read 82232. I had the nut full house on the board, but any pocket pair higher than my 8s had me beat. I just felt like he was betting entirely too high if he had something better than me. I checked on over to him and he thought for about 30 seconds and fired out a $125k bet. I wasn't nervous or anything and everything in my head was telling me that he had AK. I was up about $350k when the hand started and if I lost this hand, more than half of that was going to be gone. But I had to just forget about the money for a second and narrow down the situation.

I think I threw up in my mouth and I nonchalantly tossed in five $25k chips and made the $125,000 call. He smiled and said good hand and mucked. I never even had to show my hand to the rest of the table since he outright folded. I scooped the $450k pot and tipped the dealer $800. After that hand I was up almost $600k for the session. I was exhausted and wanted to leave. I had been up for about 30 hours, but I was destroying the game and I didn't know if I would ever have this opportunity ever again. So I gave everyone a two hour warning that I would be taking off then. They sort of all agreed, so we decided to up the limits for the last hour and played $3k/$6k and $500/$1k PLO and NL.

Even though the limits were maxed out, the action pretty much never changed. I went on a rush and won the majority of the hands in the final 45 minutes of play and we called it a night.

I won $985,000.

A number that to this day still hasn't processed given my company that night and the element I was in. But it just goes to show you that it's still the same game. There's still flush draws that are missed and suck outs that you can't control. It's still the same game one way or the other. The stakes just define how much money you may have or the risk you are willing to take on that day. That was obviously the highest I had ever played and it stayed that way. Honestly, after that first hand I won, the money value kind of just disappeared from my thoughts. I just looked at them as chips and I had never been more focused in my career. You just get into a rhythm sometimes in life and when you're really good at something, it just makes sense. Poker made sense to me.

I was delusional by this point and had been awake for almost 36 hours. But I had to get the fuck out of this town after that session. I had Bellagio arrange me a private jet to get my ass back to Chicago or I knew I would have hot hands with my recent winnings and lose all of it back betting sports or playing blackjack. I needed time to recuperate and remember what normal life felt like and looked like. My attitude didn't really change much, I threw a few grand in my jeans for pocket cash and a limo was waiting for me outside to head back to the airport and to the private hanger.

My bankroll was just over $1.7 million.

"The only thing I know about luck and a winning streak, is that it breathes just like us and it will change its course of action when you least expect it."

It Comes & It Goes-

I just laid there. Couldn't tell exactly if I had caught some second wind or was just numb. I had been awake almost 40 hours at this point. The sky outside the window was pitched black and I asked the pilots to turn the cabin lights down to a small dim. I knew that I wasn't going to be able to fall asleep, but still. My thoughts, mind and just reaction to what had taken place the last 24 hours, left me speechless. That's definitely a hard task to accomplish too. The stewardess brought me a glass of whiskey on the rocks since I looked sad as she put it. I just laughed it off and enjoyed my drink and embraced the usual view.

Every time I went back and forth from Vegas to home, especially on trips that I won substantial amounts of money, when the plane landed back in Chicago I almost felt foreign. There were no palm trees or groups of women. The air wasn't thin and there was no limousine waiting for me. Especially in the wintertime when there would be snow on the ground and not immense heat hitting my face. There were no mountains surrounding me and the days seemed to pass at a faster rate than those in Vegas. But it was home. It was always good to come back home.

I drove back to my mother's intending on spending the night and head down to Champaign to see my friends and Mindy the following morning. And hopefully stay the week. I missed all of them a lot. The more I thought about it, maybe it was the recent victory I had but I wanted to marry her. I did. I understood that they were all still in college, but it's not like we would run off to Vegas to get it done right away. We would stay engaged for a while until we established ourselves and she found a job. But again, it was just something that was passing through my mind here and there. Having love in life is so important to me.

I got back to my mother's and spent some time with her. One thing I never really did was be open about dollar amounts with my parents. I tried to keep it under wraps from them as much as possible. It wasn't easy at times when I would come home with backpacks full of cash. I felt like they worried enough about me, even with me talking to both of them on a daily basis pretty much. So you never really found me bragging about big wins or losses. I just held them to myself pretty much. I talked about recent things with my friends since the hands and thoughts were constantly running through my head. I did change up the amounts of the pots and what my bankroll was at. They knew what I was doing for a living, and that was enough information for anyone.

I slept for about an hour on the plane and it was probably the smartest decision for me to collapse and go to sleep. I was supposed to drive down to Champaign that morning pretty early, but the thought of driving two hours on the road after being up for two days straight at this point just made me want to vomit. I think I fell asleep before I even had a chance to make a final decision.

Waking up on mornings when I knew I didn't have an entire casino below my suite was always the most peaceful of its kind. Whether it was waking up in my own home or down in Champaign, the thought of being able to not have the ability to gamble was a safe feeling. A feeling of reality for once, sometimes it was all I essentially needed. I didn't feel rushed like I had to get up and get ready and get moving to make that day worth it. I could roll around in bed or make breakfast or watch T.V. I could do things that normal people did on their weekends or off days.

While my mother made me scrambled eggs that morning and I tried to act like I was paying attention to our conversation, all I could think about was the $1.7 million in my security box back at Bellagio. How all of that cash and life changing money was simply nestled through a key lock in its own tiny prison cell smaller than a shoebox. Just how bad I wanted to go back and gamble somehow someway. I wanted to go all out too. I wanted to bet sports, put $500k on a blackjack table, challenge guys in poker to the same stakes I had been playing. My almost $1 million win the day before made me feel like I could do anything I wanted at this point. But, money and Vegas can make you believe that reality doesn't exist. It's just a fairy tale land with very expensive tickets to ride their rides.

My long trip home and time away from Vegas and its ways was cut short. My psyche and degeneracy couldn't wait another second to gamble. I hadn't been home longer than 15 hours before I was en route back to Midway Airport. You would think that I would be back on another private jet, but I only had $2k in cash on me and I didn't have any credit or debit cards back then. So I kind of forced myself to take a regular flight that night. It felt good to be back in an airport. The last few times I had flown, I was coming on and off the jet way in private jets. I was jumping on and off private planes and into limousines for a few trips now that I forgot about the people at Southwest that knew me by my first name.

"Back to Vegas, Mr. Woolworth?"

"For now, please."

I hadn't been to that counter for weeks it felt like and they still knew who I was. I loved flying. I loved everything about it. I loved the mystery of who you were going to see walking through the airport or the random drink you might find at the airport bar. Airports are like one of the only places in the world where you can lie about anything you want and you will never see the person again. Maybe I always waited for that random person to sit down at the chair next to me while I waited for my flight. Because I knew they would love to hear about what I did for a living once I told them I gambled for a profession. It wasn't a usual response you heard from other travelers. Immediately they became curious and responsive. It was really those few hours of curiousness that kept me going sometimes.

My flight was only about an hour after I bought my ticket. Just enough time to buy a drink, catch up on scores in baseball and the NBA and board the plane. On back to Vegas I went.

The wheels touched down and I was in my usual pose of staring out the window and holding onto my drink until the last second. I turned my phone back on as the brakes grinded as hard as they could and my eyes rested staring out the window at the strip in the distant view that I fell in love with just 18 months prior. Bellagio was right where I left it as we taxied in to our gate.

I was antsy and practically salivating and speed walking through the airport to get to the taxi line. I usually only packed one bag so I never had to stop at baggage claim. I was off the plane and out the door for the majority of my trips in less than ten minutes. It was around 8pm local time and I was back in Vegas. I guess I couldn't get enough. The cab driver did his usual speech and I think I cut him off and told him to just take me to Bellagio.

We pulled up to the circle driveway and Santiago the valet manager spotted me and gave me his hellos and asked why I was rolling around in taxis. We shared a laugh and I walked into the lobby and up to the front desk. I asked if they had any suites available and she ran my player's card. A player's card is a card that you give the floor man in charge before you gamble at all. Whether you are playing poker, or in the pits or on the slots, all of it qualifies. Then they monitor what you're doing and how long you are playing for. You accumulate points and that way they can always keep track as to what kind of gambler you are. They can classify you into certain types of levels that will in return help you get free rooms, meals and shows etc.

I qualified where I could have anything I ever wanted at this point. She set me up with one of the presidential suites and I made my usual walk through the casino and up to one of the highest floors in the hotel. The anticipation of what your room was going to look like was always a feeling to look forward to. All of them were somehow different and unique in their own little ways. Even though I didn't spend much time in them unless I was sleeping, I always did a walk through so I could at least appreciate the free room for a few minutes.

I opened up my bar and made myself a vodka red bull and stared out at the lights. That view was definitely something I never got tired of looking at. Sometimes my room would face the east or sometimes the west. But Vegas' capacity is literally surrounded by mountains. Safe to say that I have seen the entire 360 degree view of that enclosed town constructed by the devil himself.

I walked up to the cage and asked for my security box. She confirmed my identity and I took out $500k in $25k chips and stashed them into my pocket. I walked on over to the poker room to see if there was any action going on that would be able to sustain my needs right now but there wasn't. The highest game was $40/$80 and I guess it became a limit that wasn't worth my time anymore. Since just a few days prior I was playing stakes almost a hundred times that size. I placed $25k on an NBA game and made my way on over to the blackjack tables. I found one that wasn't occupied and there was my favorite floor manager Mikey. He shook my hand and said that he had heard about my big win in Bobby's Room and it had kind of been the talk of the casino over the last couple of days. We talked about it briefly and he had a few questions of his own. I answered as always and got to work.

I requested two bodyguards since the only open table in the high limit area was out in plain view for the public to see and on the corner of one of the busiest walkways in Vegas. I waited for the two of them to show up and I bought in for $475k. I ordered another drink and put my feet up on the chair next to me. I knew the one bodyguard. He played football in college and was a bouncer for a couple of nightclubs before ending up at Bellagio. He was about 6'8 and weighed close to 325 pounds. His name was Jack. The other gentleman was new at Bellagio. He was a little bigger than Jack, but he was African American and his name was Garret. Both of them stood behind me with one facing outwards towards the tourists as they passed on by and the other facing me for my protection. Sometimes I would turn around and there would be a few curious souls trying to look past the soldiers behind me to get a view. The chips I had in front of me were colors that the public wasn't used to. They were used to seeing the red, green and black colored chips, resembling $5, $25 and $100. So my bright white, yellows and purples were quite noticeable and eye catching.

Of the $475k I bought in with, I left $250k in $25k chips, another $200k in $5ks and the remaining $25k in $1ks. I started out betting $2k a hand to get warmed up and in little to no time I was on a heater and up about $50k. The double downs were working for me and I hit a blackjack on a $30k bet for a $45k payout. But decided to press it the following hand and lost a $55k bet to a nuisance discovered 20 against my made 19. After an hour I think I was only up about $10k. I was pretty focused, but was also living on a new high that I had never felt before. I was self-consciously still caught up on my big win. It apparently wasn't affecting my current play. I thought my degeneracy would have pulled out the balls in me to bet $100k a hand by now. But it was just another blackjack session, so far.

All shit hit the fan after I ordered a shot of patron and I was about six drinks deep. I was down about $20k, but I started to bet between $10k & $30k a hand, so that negative was irrelevant. Blackjack is weird at times. There had been times where I would lose fifteen hands in a row, then a new dealer would jump in and I would win fifteen hands in a row. For this session I was pretty consistent with the streaks and flow of the game. I bet $15k on a hand and was dealt two 8s against the dealers 5. I decided to split them and threw out another $15k and took a sip of my drink. She threw me another 8 and I put out another $15k. So I had three hands out there. The first 8 she gave me a 2 for a 10, I doubled down and put down another $15k. I had $60k out there at this point and she gave me a 7. So my first hand read 17. The next 8 she gave me a king and I had 18. My last 8 she gave me a 3 and I doubled down again. She gave me a meaningless 4 for 15. I had $75k out there hanging in the balance. She panned out a 7 for 12 and an 8 for 20. Scooping me and my $75k and starting me on a major downswing, to say the least.

I still had about $400k in front of me and increased my bet to $20k a hand. I went on a nice thirty minute run where I won back $130k with a couple of blackjacks. Cruising along I found bets to sit and stand at $50k a hand for a little while. It was a lot of back and forth and I wasn't up or down more than $200k the entire time which is interesting given the stakes. I went to take a piss and picked up another $500k from my box and made my way back. With close to $1 million in front of me, pretty much all of my profit from my winnings the other day, I felt more comfortable after taking a walk and brought my bets back down to $10k a hand and sort of started over. My bodyguards switched out since about six hours had passed and I tipped each of them $1k for their time and I got two new ones. I was probably ten drinks deep at this point and getting hungry. But I decided to order another drink and keep on playing.

I hit a downswing and was down $300k and I hadn't bet more than $25k a hand for about an hour or so. I put out a $75k bet and got dealt two 9s against the dealers 4. I decided to split them and received face cards for both giving me 19, the dealer tucked up a

4 and a queen, giving her 18 and I scooped both. I bet $100k on the next hand and got an ugly draw, a 16 against the dealers jack. It's one of the worst scenarios possibly given to a blackjack player, so I hit and got a 3 giving me a hopeful 19. I screamed out 7 and the dealer turned over a 7 giving her 17 and just like that I won back $250k in two hands. I decided to take a break and get some sushi. I walked over to the sports book first to see if I won my $25k bet from earlier on and I did. I asked for $10k in cash and the rest in chips and pocketed my winnings.

I left my $950k on the table where I was so that the bodyguards didn't have to walk around with me. I trusted it to be there when I got back and the table was at this point roped off too, plus they still guarded the table while I was gone. I came back about an hour later and got back to work with a new drink in my hand. I decided to switch over to captain and cokes and was probably on my 12th drink for the session and back to being intoxicated. The next few hours didn't go as planned.

I had been playing for about ten hours at this point and my average bet was $30k according to the floor man. I was down $500k and kind of just looked at the money in front of me as profit from a poker night that I will never forget. If anything it's like free money given the lineup that I was playing against that night. I should've gone broke and never had this money. Maybe that's just me being optimistic, but still. I was fully willing to gamble like a crack head with this remaining $500k and be alright with the outcome. I would still have $800k left in my box if that were the case if I lost all of this.

I still had a small crowd past my bodyguards watching me play. Some would even stand on the other side of the pits behind the tables in front of me for a more distant view if they could see. My 99 diamond watch on my left wrist just sat there flashing itself off. Every once and a while I would look down at it to see what time it was, but it was like time never moved when I was playing blackjack. I was just there in the moment.

I bet $80k on the next hand and was dealt two face cards but unfortunately so did the dealer. I left my bet out there and this time I was dealt blackjack, getting paid out $120k. I bet the table max of $125k on the next hand, and was dealt an 11 against the dealers 7. I said fuck it and doubled down and got a 6. Was hoping she would turn over a face card and we would tie and I would bring my bet back down. With $250k out there, she turned over a black ace for 18 and scooped up my chips like they were nickels and dimes. Shit.

I had $155k left in front of me and decided to call it a night. I dropped back about $850k, but with the sports bet it was a fat loss around $825k for the session. I tipped the bodyguards behind me $1k each and walked towards the cage. I tried to convince myself that everything was alright. I wasn't mad or upset I guess, that's just how gambling and blackjack goes. You win some and you lose some. I understood the amount I just lost, but maybe it just hadn't clicked yet either. It's not like it was my entire bankroll, I pretty much was up $150k the last two sessions of gambling instead of $1 million. It was part of the game, part of the life. I didn't know if it was a good thing or a bad thing that I didn't have any feeling. It was dangerous that

I was used to playing the highest stakes this early on and that I may have lost the appreciation of playing regular high stakes poker and being satisfied from it. I found it extremely mentally difficult to convince myself to go back and play $100/$200 or $200/$400 after betting $125k on blackjack hands and calling $125k on a river bet by one of poker's greatest players in the world at that time. But it's all mental in the end. You have to learn how to win at all levels and you also have to learn how to lose at all levels too. With my biggest win and biggest loss being in back to back sessions, yet I am still up $150k between the two, I should be happy with myself.

It had been a while since I just walked up and down the strip. I had a full stomach and all the gamble out of me for a while I think. I stopped at the bar and grabbed another drink and started to walk north on the strip. Figured I would do some type of loop where I got down to the Wynn and crossed the street and worked my back to PH and across the street on back to Bellagio. Even though action was kicking up because the WSOP was underway, I just needed a night away from everything. Whether I was still in Vegas or not, I needed time away from the tables.

Even with the sun down behind the mountains, it was still 100 degrees out and my drink was gone before I even hit the next casino's property. I stopped at one of those outdoor bars and found some type of huge margarita that was at least 25 oz. but entirely fulfilling. The rest of my night would consist of random conversations with girls, people watching, about five more drinks, viewing a fight, denying hookers, thinking about my life and Mindy, that I was one tick under a millionaire and that I was still one of the biggest gamblers in the country.

But I was at the beginning stage of a downfall that was going to eventually terminate me, my life and the people around me. The next 12 months became a long goodbye to all of this. But for now, I was alright.

"But bad luck makes for life changing stories, I promise."

Nine Weeks in 08'

Up to this point in my career, I was safe. Nothing really too stupid had happened yet. I never got hurt or was ever put in any harm. Given the amount of traveling I was doing and mixed in with the weight of money I had, the roses always seemed to bloom on my side of town. I made sure that I was protected at times where I had substantial amounts of money in front of me. Bellagio never said no if I requested bodyguards or even police escorts to the airport like I was the president or back to another hotel nearby. But, stupid things in life do happen. Not just as ingredients in my poker career, but sometimes things in life can become entirely more overwhelming. The personal side of things can send your career in a direction you aren't prepared for. Especially when you feel like there is no way out. I am not too much of a religious man, but I do believe that God was trying to tell me something when I went through the devastating events I am about to relive in such a short timeframe.

I was in the small blind with pocket kings and only had ten big blinds left. We were three handed and I just lost half my stack to James a few hands prior. The blinds were huge, $50k/$100k. He had been quite aggressive in the later part of the tournament actually. I figured that if I limped in and he raised me, which he was doing three times the size of the big blind quite often in those scenarios, that I would obviously go all in and pick up some chips if not double up if he called. He checked his option this time and the flop came up 972. A pretty dry flop given the element. I decided to check and he bet the minimum of $100k. I made it $250k to go and he went all in and I snap called. He flipped over 97 for top two pair, devastating my pocket kings. The turn and the river were burned and turned and I was out in third place just like that. James won the tournament just two hands later. As I have previously mentioned this tournament before, I should have won it. Mindy skipped her college final to drive up and see me play, all of my friends were there and more importantly it was the first time my father had ever seen me play cards. I exited the studio and made my way to the back of the boat wanting to chuck my phone in the lake so that I didn't have to talk to anyone for as long as I wanted. To this day I still wonder what that celebration would have been like if I had won that tournament. I'm still not over it, probably never will be able to accept that meltdown that I did that day. It's only now that I realize how special that moment should have been had I done it soberly and professionally. That was April 28th.

A couple of weeks later I was driving up I-294 northbound completely hammered. Not as bad as usual though. I had just met up with some friends at a strip club on the south side of Chicago. As I was driving home, I was following a flatbed semi-truck that had some loose pieces of steel on its back apparently. Without warning and just as I was changing lanes, a piece of steel about eight feet long flew off the back of the truck and I rolled over it going 70 miles per hour. Swerving uncontrollably and rolling over it, along came another one that I collided with as well. I finally gained control with no injuries and pulled off to the side of the road. The flatbed didn't have a clue as to what had just happened and kept on going peacefully into the night. I turned my car off and opened the door to see of any damage. I was so intoxicated that I didn't check my mirror before I opened my door and opened it directly into a semi in the right lane. I was pushed back into my car by the force of it going as fast it was. Fortunately, somehow my door and I were untouched. It was an awful scare to my conscious and life as if the previous sixty seconds weren't enough already. I had no damage to the outer exterior of my car. There was a long black streak of liquid running from the highway where I was to where my car was parked. My oil tank had been destroyed and now my car refused to start. I had to have a friend come pick me up and get the car towed back to a local shop by my house. The following morning when they opened up, I had to push it into the shop so that they could look at it. The under carriage looked as if someone had beat the fuck out of it for days. My hemi engine was obliterated along with other repairs. Thankfully I had insurance and the $9,700 check my insurance wrote me went straight to the company that fixed it all for me. That was the middle of May.

My car was out of commission for about a week since they had to put a whole new engine in it. When I got it back, I still had about $20k left at Majestic which was the casino where I had just gotten third place in. They had some random high stakes NL game going on and I wanted to pick up the cash before I headed back out to Vegas for the WSOP in a couple of weeks. So it all kind of timed out. I got my car back and went for a ride.

I played in the game for seven hours and won $5k. I intentionally wore a hoody and covered my head to divert any type of attention from the public. It worked but it didn't. When I was finished, I grabbed my backpack and headed towards the cage. The ladies there recognized me and paid me out the $8k in chips I had from the game plus the $20k I left with the vault from the tournament. They paid me out in full, all in hundreds and I made my way towards the parking garage. It was the first and only time I had never valeted my car or walked out without any bodyguards. I was a few spots away from my car when two men in masks, wearing dark gloves, and dressed in all black stepped out from behind the SUV parked next to my car. They both raised automatic weapons about three feet in length between my eyes and told me not to move another foot. The one came up and took the bag off my shoulder but without any force or anything. Neither one of them touched me. Right before they ran away, they told me to give them my Rolex. But the kicker was that my hoody was covering it and it was never exposed. Only way they would have known I had it on was they either saw me inside the casino, or someone let them know when I was leaving with the cash, that I was also wearing a Rolex under my hoody. So I didn't really know who set this up or anything. Unfortunately, I didn't know who to trust anymore after that. They could have been friends of mine and that's why they didn't want to hurt me. I knew plenty of guys that owed tons of cash to other gamblers and bookies. Could have really been anyone under those masks in the corner of that parking garage. With the value of the Rolex and the cash, I was out about $35k. Not a loss that I had never experienced before or anything while gambling. It was if anything the most polite robbery I had ever seen before. I could have easily been shot for no reason or killed. When they were finally out of sight, I continued on to my car, which they didn't vandalize thank God and headed home. I acted as if nothing ever happened, nor did I mention it to anyone, ever. I was in shock for a while, but was just happy that nothing harmful had occurred. It took me five years to ever go back to a Chicago casino ever again because of that night. But I survived, all that matters. That was the end of May.

Being summertime and all, Mindy was home from school. It was nice having her around. But of course there were times that I did miss that therapeutic drive down to Champaign every once and a while. It was my quiet time to think over things. I thought I was falling completely in love with her and was definitely thinking more about our future together. But again, it was hard to make valid life decisions when you were intoxicated every day. We were leaving a movie around 9pm and when I turned my blackberry back on, I had at least 40 notifications from people all over the Chicago land poker community. Mixed with texts, missed calls and voicemails, no one would tell me what the fucking problem was. They just kept on saying that something awful has happened and to please call me back and all this other shit. In the midst of me still scrolling through all of these recent messages, my phone rang and it was my buddy.

"Nick, did you hear about Eric? I guess he was on his motorcycle without a helmet on and some lady turned left in front of him and he went head first into her passenger door and was flown a hundred feet."

After what seemed like an hour long pause he finally let out the news.

"He didn't make it."

Right there in the middle of the movie theatre lobby I dropped to my knees. The tears flowed without warning and I couldn't help myself. He was if anything my closest friend in the poker world. I was with him just a couple days before at a Cubs game and we were having a great time. He was a successful gentleman who was in his mid-30s, CFO of a company, great poker player and looking to get engaged in the coming few months. He was just that guy where when he walked in the room, everyone else was in a better mood because he was around. To this day I can still hear his laugh and can remember the times we spent together. Just a prime example that life can just end at any given second and it's still so hard to believe he's not alive anymore. He died on June 18th, just a couple weeks after I got robbed. For the weeks to come I found myself just tearing up randomly while playing. Or I was calling his phone which was immediately going to his voicemail and I would just listen to his voice. I missed him and I still do. Always will.

I had to go back to Vegas. I hadn't been there for a couple of weeks. Eric's passing made me kind of closed off from the world for a little while and since Mindy was home, we were doing things around the city for the majority of our time. I had different intentions on going back to Vegas this time around though. That last time that Eric and I were together at the Cubs game, I told him how much I loved her and what she meant to me. And that I wanted to propose to her. He told me a story about a girl he once knew when he was my age and he felt the same way. But it freaked him out and he actually broke up with her instead. He knew he wasn't ready then and wanted to establish himself in life before he made such a commitment. And even though he said he regrets not doing it, he still had to find ways to deal with that decision as life progressed. One of his last pieces of advice that he gave me was to just do it. If I felt that it was right, then pick out the ring and plan on how you want to do it. So, Mindy had a sister that lived in Hawaii and I figured I would surprise her with a trip out there and then do it on the beach sometime at sunset. Poetic I know and maybe cheesy, but we had been talking about going out there for quite some time. What better time to go than the middle of July. I booked the trip to go out there the second week in July. I needed a vacation. The only time her and I ever traveled together was trips to Vegas. She loved the town and everything was free for me. It was just convenient if anything. I felt that a real vacation made sense given the last few weeks I had endured.

I got back on a plane and headed back to Vegas. They had plenty of jewelry stores in the hotels and the malls for me to choose a ring from. We had talked about children's names and where we might live someday, but never about a ring and all of the precious things must it have to make a woman happy. What kind, size and everything in between. I figured I would pick out one that I loved the most, try to spend less than $20k and if she wanted to exchange it for something else we could figure it out together down the road.

After a long two days and probably thirty jewelry stores later, I found a two carat gem worth about $19k and couldn't have been happier. I was eager, excited and just happy in general. Given the negative that had been going on the last few weeks, my mind was finally at a calm spot and I couldn't wait another two days to get home. So I made a decision that changed my life forever. I flew home 48 hours early.

When I landed at Midway, a buddy of mine called me and asked if I wanted to go to the White Sox game that night. I figured that since I was just a few minutes from the stadium and had about an hour to get there, I would join him. I called Mindy to let her know that I was back in town, but she didn't answer. We had decent seats, about 15 rows up from the third base dugout. It had been a while since I had seen him, so we had some beers and some laughs and it was a great night for a ball game. About two hours into the game we began to take notice to an obnoxious couple one section over and about ten rows down. They were drunk and being loud and inappropriate. I didn't really think anything of it yet. I texted Mindy again and she still didn't respond. She was usually pretty good about keeping in contact with me when I was out of town too. My eyes decided to finally adjust to this couple again. The more I paid attention, it clicked. With the engagement ring in my pocket, there she was with another guy. Right there in front of me. I pointed it out to my friend so that he could somehow convince me that wasn't her, but he couldn't disagree. Everything inside my body died. It was a new type of feeling I had never experienced before. All the air was sucked out of my chest and I couldn't do anything else but stare. That same smile I fell in love with was now rested upon another man. I snapped a couple of pictures with my phone and told my buddy let's get the fuck out of here. I couldn't stand the sight anymore.

I dropped him off and all the emotions built up inside of me just let loose. I stopped at a liquor store and got a fifth of jack. I went to a random pond by my old house and sat on the hood of my car with the engagement ring as my company. I just sat there under the moon that followed me around and drank half the bottle and cried. I called my father and he couldn't believe it either given the run of bad luck I had been living through these last few weeks. I gathered myself up, she still didn't answer her phone and I headed back home.

When I woke up, I just remember laying there. She still hadn't responded to any of my texts or calls. It was like I was dead to her. Or maybe she got too drunk and her phone died and she just hasn't woken up yet. I guess it could be anything at this point. That's another thing about that life I once had, simply anything was always a possibility. I couldn't get the image out of my head of what I had seen the night before. It didn't help that I took pictures on my blackberry and I kept on going back to look at them either. The image I have of her and the sadness I had to see her with someone else convinced me pretty much. I didn't even pack a bag, but I headed back to the airport and back to Vegas to return the ring. It was the morning of July 2nd.

In a span of just 64 days I went through almost every drastic event you can come up with. I ruined a moment with my friends and father that I believe had I won that tournament that all of the negatives to follow may not have happened. I would have been somewhere else that night than driving home on that highway when I got into the car accident. I would've been doing something else that night instead of picking up my remaining $20k and wouldn't have been robbed. First place for that tournament was $180k. I would have had a bank wire to an account or another casino. I wouldn't have left anything there. Eric's whole life would have been different. He and I would have been together at different points if I won that tournament between the day of and the day of his death. Things would have been altered and he may still be alive.

Then I truly think that if she would have seen me win that tournament right in front of her that she would have thought differently about my career and my future as a poker player. She would have been able to have seen that success and potential I had in the game with her own eyes. And she may have never cheated on me.

So, I lost success, a terrifying car accident, got robbed, close friend passed away and I caught the love of my life cheating on me in public with the engagement ring in my pocket. It was safe to say that I should just get the hell out of Chicago as fast as I could.

I was never mad at her. I never showed her the pictures I had taken that night at the game for evidence. When we finally talked I told her that I had seen everything. I described what they were wearing and where they were sitting and that it was best to just be honest with me. We broke up and she was Facebook official with him in just two weeks. I never told her about the ring. It was returned back to the jewelry store in Vegas with a drink in my hand of course. I told the guy at the counter that life sometimes just has a way of talking to you. And that this belongs on the finger of someone else.

I was exhausted and drained, both mentally and physically. I didn't know what I was doing with my life now. She was really the only type of motivation I had for a future because to me she was my future. I used to call her my sense of reality and she hated it. Because she thought that she didn't mean anything to me when I wasn't with her. I would fly off to Vegas and do all of this unbelievable shit and then come home to her and all of that fairy tale stuff would go away. I felt normal again with her. Which is something I really needed. That sense of balance was very important to me in my life. Once it was gone, I didn't have anything else to do really in that sense.

I didn't have a plan. I was pissed at the world and disappointed in myself because of it. But I couldn't figure out why. I had been in the spotlight for what felt like such a long time and now I didn't have much to go back to anymore in Chicago. I felt like even through the historical things I had been through, and the praise I received from the poker community constantly, that I wouldn't be feeling the way that I did. That I would be happy living the life I was. But I was just putting on a happy face for the last few months as the traumatic events kept happening to me one after the other. Problem with all of this was my closest friends thought that everything was ok. They thought that I was doing just fine emotionally because I had money and I was successful in my profession. But given the recent events, I was by no means successful in life. A lot of people back home looked at me as a piece of shit because they assumed I was fucking hookers, my stories were lies and I was just living in some never never land all the time. I was constantly inviting people out to Vegas. I mean that literally. I wanted people to be able to see me and sit next to me and be with me. I was alone 99% of the time I was out there. I don't think anyone really understands what that means or what that feels like. If I could just have someone there with me through all of it, I believe that I would still be in that profession as a gambler. But at the same time I wanted to be able to give anyone I cared about the full on experience of what it was like to be me. To show them and be the gambler that I was because part of me truly knew that this wasn't going to last forever. I wanted to have the chance to capture any moments they could possibly see.

The only place on the planet that would make this shit go away where I was ok with losing was Vegas. Being at the poker table or playing blackjack. Or walking around the strip with a long island iced tea in my hand enjoying the scenery. These were the only things that were going to make me forget about these horrific and life changing events. Even if it was for just a few hours at a time where I wasn't constantly thinking about them. I could use that time of peace to focus on me and my game and whatever the future had in store for me. I had to keep moving forward somehow. I still had about $875k as my bankroll.

Vegas was about to prove to me though why they build casinos and that the house always wins. That this town was built because of tourists and individuals who extended their stay and thought that they could beat the house. Guys like me would eventually have their luck run out.

"If you do not change direction, you may eventually end up where you are heading."

Armageddon-

It was 124 degrees. The middle of July was always the hottest time to be in Vegas. Sometimes it felt refreshing since it was dry heat finding your skin. I was so used to the humid Chicago summers that this was enjoyable most of the time. Since the casinos are set at the standard 72 degrees, sometimes you were almost stepping in and out of a fifty degree difference between inside the casinos and outside.

The limo was black as always. I don't know, I always requested a black one because I felt that white limos were reserved for weddings or something. We all know that getting married wasn't a scenario in my life any time soon given the recent occurrences back home.

But, I was back. I was back for good. I didn't really have any intention on going back to Chicago at this point. All of my friends were home from school and I just spent the whole summer with them. Mindy was the main reason of going back and forth and she chose to not be a part of my life anymore. This was all I had for now. I saw it to be a perfect time with the World Series of Poker coming to an end, to just focus again on cash games and what I was good at. Just kill them with success as my father would have always said it. Just execute them with your stats and results. Let your bat do the talkin' in baseball language that is.

I had a discussion with one of the head managers for the Bellagio and told him that I planned on staying out here until I couldn't take it anymore. I understood that asking to stay in a presidential suite for 60 days was ludicrous. But if I could just have a standard room for the next 60 days and go from there that would be plentiful. I mean, that's only like a $15k value. The suites I stayed in, some of those cost $8k a night and more. Seemed like a rational trade. I was hoping that I was going to focus and play poker. But you never know with this town and once I started drinking. He gave me just as I requested and set me up with an ordinary room facing the pond for free. It had been quite some time since I had stayed in a room that didn't have a full kitchen in it or 30' ceilings. This was home for a while, or so I hoped. But, I realized I didn't need all of that. I was on the 19th floor and still had the same view of whoever was staying just a few floors above me in some flawless suite. It's all irrelevant in the end. This moment proves that. Here I am in this 500 square foot room with the same beautiful sight of Vegas' skyline beginning to emerge as the sun goes down, but I could still see the same thing in the 2800 square foot suite just above. It's all about the view on life. It's all about how you want to see the scenery just outside your window to make you appreciate that moment.

Sushi, I needed it. It had been a while since I had some since Mindy didn't enjoy it. That's another thing. I'm a foodie. Being in Vegas and going to all of these beautiful restaurants, I became obsessed with food and dinners, which I have previously stated. I wish I could find a new restaurant in Chicago to go to every week if possible. But it's easier said than done. I was going to do everything that I could to distract myself from the fatiguing last few months I had just sustained. When the plane took off to come here, I started to cry. It was some picture-perfect sunset, unlike one I had ever seen before. Everything had just kind of hit me all at once. A lot of it had to do with her. I truly missed Eric too. I wanted to be successful for him now. He was always so supportive in everything I had done with poker and my life as a whole. And he would've supported this too. I found some spicy scallop and tuna and feasted until my stomach was complete.

I felt like I was in Vegas for the first time all over again. I was motivated to be back. It had been a while since I had played any type of high stakes cash games, so I knew that I needed to be realistic and understand that this is my life and I need to start treating this more like a profession than a degenerate hobby. I had an opportunity to be something in this game and I needed to appreciate that. I needed to love the gift that I had inside of me for this game.

I did an overview of the room and saw that the $100/$200 game was seven handed just as I loved it. Since it was midnight and dinnertime had passed, I knew that these guys were locked in for at least six hours. I told the floor man to save me a seat and he looked at me like he had seen a ghost. Terry was one of the top floor managers for the Bellagio's Poker Room and could drink scotch with the best of them. He shook my hand and I made my way to the cage and to my box that I hadn't opened in almost two months. I had about $50k in cash that I brought with me, but I wanted to keep it that way and just maneuver with the chips I had stashed. I cracked open the box and there was a scattered amount of chips. I counted them out and it came out to $814k. I took $14k and headed back to the poker room and bought into the $100/$200 game with all of it, but asked for $5k in $25 chips.

I felt like I was back in my element. I was mantled a few steps above the rest of the poker room and the 25+ tables below. I was in plain view for the rest of the world to see me sitting in seat seven. I put my headphones on and sweated the baseball game on a television above my head that I bet $1k on. I was just finally at peace with myself. I was right where I was meant to be.

I got into a nice hand that would play out the way that it did anywhere on any poker table at any limit. I looked down at JTcc and raised to $200. The player to my left called and the button three bet to $300, the big blind called and I called along with the gentleman to my left. The flop was 983 and I bet out $100 on my open ended straight draw. The player to my left raised to $200 and the button three bet to $300. I called the $300 as did the guy to my left. The turn was the 4c, giving me a flush draw as well now, so I decided to bet out $200. The guy to my left called and the button called. The river was an offset queen, giving me the nuts with a straight and I bet out $200. The guy to my left called and the button raised me to $400. I instantly put him on pocket queens for top set. So I three bet to $600 and he figured it out. He called in disgust and I flipped my hand over in triumph. He showed his pocket queens briefly and mucked and I scooped the $3k plus pot. It was a noble start already.

A few hours would pass and it was six in the morning. I hadn't had a drink all night which wasn't like me. Not even at dinner. I won $5,600 for the session and decided to call it quits. I also won the baseball bet I made, so all in all it was a good day.

I made my way back to my room and I was confused. I didn't know what it was like to be sober and up at this time of the morning. Not feeling drunk or having that whiskey on my breath sent confusion through my conscious. But the sunrise was the same; the view didn't change at all. So what was the difference? I didn't know and I didn't have an answer.

I was an asshole and I called Mindy. Chances are she wouldn't answer, but I just wanted to hear her voicemail. Part of me felt abandoned. I wasn't ready to see the sights that I did that night in the midst of what I was going through already in life. As expected, the voicemail kicked in. A few seconds after the beep, I finally found the bravery to tell her that I missed her and I hung up.

Waking up without that cotton mouth feeling and sense of exhaustion was different for me. I didn't feel like complete shit for once. I woke up feeling upright and even went downstairs to the spa and got an hour long massage from some ridiculously sexy Asian lady. She almost made me cry it felt so good. I grabbed a greasy burger and when I was finished I headed to the poker room during the midafternoon. There was my favorite game and miraculously, I think his name was Sy, but he was still in the same seat I left him at just ten hours before. The best part was he looked stuck, so he wasn't going anywhere. I bought in for the usual $5k and found myself in the usual seven seat.

"Seven and seven please."

I lasted a mere 24 hours of no alcohol intake and that was it for me. From here on out, I would be drinking. Either in my hand, rested below me in a cup holder or waiting for a refill. It never tasted as good as it did now being as hot as it was outside. But I was still going to focus on just playing poker and taking it from there.

Three weeks had passed. I had grown a full beard, was up $125k playing in the $100/$200 and $200/$400 games and betting sports and feeling fine. I was eating alright every day and trying to stay in the correct mindset. All of this was still new to me again. I was winning which was great, but I was highly depressed and still gloomy about everything. I had a few nights where I didn't remember coming home to my room, but for the most part I was just a standard drunk every night. I became a fan of getting back massages at the table while I was playing. It kind of kept me well-balanced. Sure it costs me about $400 a night, but was worth it I felt since I was winning $10-$15k a day.

The first thing that I can remember that triggered it was a hand in poker that I had probably lost a dozen times in my life. Just the usual I have aces and he has kings ordeal. But before you know it the dealer is shifting your opponent the pot instead of you. You hate it every time, but it's just part of the game. But for whatever reason this time it pissed me off. I was up $2,300 early on into the session, but I decided that after being in Vegas for three weeks, it was time that I played some blackjack.

I had walked past those tables every day and every night. I didn't look at it as a bad thing if I just stayed within some type of means. My bankroll was just a few grand under $1 million again, but that didn't mean that it was ok to sit with $100k to buy-in with either. I think I was alright if I just sat down with $10k and bet $200-$500 a hand and went from there. I colored up in the poker room's cage with the $7,500 that I had and I made my way to the pits.

I found Mikey, my favorite floor manager and we caught up for a few minutes. I sat down and threw my feet up on the chair next to me like usual. I asked for another drink and told Mikey that I wouldn't be needing bodyguards any time soon, I was going to try this new route into things.

About ten hours later I could barely keep my head up from being so exhausted and intoxicated and I was down $65k. With the cage literally twenty feet from the table, it was easy to just go there and reload if I went bust. Which I obviously did, it had been forever since I had played blackjack and even though I knew all of the correct moves and plays, didn't mean that I was going to win. I was winning in poker, but couldn't seem to get it going with blackjack. I called it a night when I was down $75k. Well, call it an afternoon. The girls were walking around in sun dresses and with bikini tops on. My phone had died and I didn't have one of my watches on, so I assumed it was the afternoon. I was stumbling and swerving through the walkway. I eventually found my room and passed out.

I woke up around midnight and felt fine I guess. I ordered some room service and for whatever reason I desired mint chocolate chip ice cream with hot fudge on top, it was my favorite. My huge BLT arrived along with it. I had a small bar inside of my stocked fridge and decided to make a drink. I found myself a lot in front of those windows looking out onto the strip. I didn't watch television much, but I did stare out that window as much as I could. And my thoughts and mind would just scatter in every which direction. It was a beautiful city filled with so much negative. The streets below were polluted with hookers and drugs. People would lose their life savings and destroy themselves over different addictions that they couldn't do anything about. But the city still looked like a fairy-tale place full of dreams. Even if it was just for a few minutes each day, I made sure that I always enjoyed the peaceful view.

Being back here again after everything had happened, maybe I started to appreciate life more. I definitely had a different view on things. I lost two of my closest friends in just a few weeks of time. Both were in awful and horrific ways that I don't wish upon anyone in this world. It stays with you forever. Those images and thoughts can haunt you if you don't treat them correctly. Mixed in with everything that was going on here, somehow I had a lot on my mind for living such an independent life. It was filled with high stakes, beautiful women always around, drugs, alcohol and awful ingredients for life. You found ways to not let it get to you. I had established a tolerance for this city that is tough to come by. I believe that in order to be any type of a successful gambler, businessman or anything in life, you have to develop a superior tolerance for your element that you put yourself into every day. Or you are entirely fucked before you even step foot in the front door. It was the occurrences in life that got to me. That made me realize that my feelings towards this game had become numb, but they still meant the world to me. I could lose $850k in a night and just hop back on a plane back to Chicago and still have a drink and talk to the person next to me the whole way. Acting as if nothing had ever happened. But dealing with the loss of someone in my life could destroy all of my internal feelings. So, is it possible that Vegas wasn't even real?

Two more weeks had passed and I wasn't doing that well. My beard had yet to be touched and I was beginning to look like I should be living up in the mountains somewhere during the wintertime hunting animals. I wasn't the same guy anymore. About ten days before I became extremely emotional at a random blackjack table betting $2k a hand and crying for about two hours straight. I wore

a hat now constantly pulled down low and my
identity was almost impossible to recognize. Unless
you were able to figure out who I was because of
the 99 diamonds I had on my watch. I was including
Bacardi for breakfast instead of orange juice and I
was down to less than $250k to my name. I had
gone 2-27 betting sports, hadn't won in blackjack in
almost a week and by the time I finally made it to a
poker table I was too intoxicated sometimes to
figure out what was going on. I started to get kicked
out and escorted out for being too intoxicated and I
was being asked politely to leave even the poker
room because of my antics.

The only way to get out of a losing streak is by
walking through it. I had to keep on playing. If I
was going to go down, I was going to go down
fighting. I wasn't going to blame it on bad decisions
or the alcohol. I had won six digits plenty of times
intoxicated, sometimes without even remembering
any of it. This was just a run of bad luck I guess.
Not that I was ever the kind of guy to believe in bad
luck though. I was always looked at it as an excuse.
I wasn't kidding when I said that I couldn't win in
anything. I even tried playing roulette and bet $500
on red for six hands in a row and somehow it came
up black every time. Do you know what the odds
are for that? About 87-1.

I started hitting on every girl, I was staying awake
for two days straight gambling and I was an asshole
to everyone that I came in contact with. Even the
individuals that had never done anything wrong to
me. The only time I talked to my parents anymore
was if I was crying and it was the early hours of the
morning. To this day I still feel horrible about what
I put them through. Everyone else's parents at my

age, all they had to worry about was if their kid was doing well at school or not. Not debating whether they had to come out to Vegas to find them and bring them home to make sure that they live to see tomorrow. My phone was notification city. I had missed calls and texts all the time from people wondering if I was alright or even alive. I just wanted to be left alone. The money was burning itself and I had no one else to blame but myself. It was just another day at this point. I was slowly destroying what I had built, but at the same time I had no reason to stop myself either. It's not like I was trying to lose either. I truly was just on a run of awful luck that I couldn't seem to get myself out of. The dollars were adding up and I felt as if my time on this planet was running out.

Seven weeks had passed and it was almost October. I was down to my last $85k and my beard was as long as I had ever seen it. It was itchy and annoying, but I didn't really have a reason to cut it either. Mixed in with the hat I was wearing constantly, I couldn't remember the last time I had been noticed by anyone. I was down to about 120 pounds and just didn't look healthy at all. I wiped out the soda and was drinking everything on the rocks for about the last month. The days became longer and my diet turned to snacks and fast food. There were no more steak dinners or sushi. The only time water touched me was in the shower. And unfortunately, the days began and ended with Mindy on my mind.

I went to my security box and pulled out the remaining three $25k chips and put them in my pocket. I had exactly $10,145 in my pocket in cash. For whatever reason the $145 was made up of seven

$20 bills and a $5 bill, don't ask. This was it for me. I made a promise to myself that I was going to sit down with all $85k and if I lost it, I was going to be on the next flight home and back to Chicago. I guess ideally the smartest thing would have been to keep the cash in my pocket since that's a lot of money and just buy in for the $75k I had in chips. But again, I clearly made poor decisions in life.

I found Mikey. Before I started the session I gave him a hug and let him know that I truly appreciated everything he had done for me in the last couple of years. I must have thanked him at least ten times. It was like I was developing my own funeral or a suicide mission that was waiting to take place. A large part of me knew that by sitting down with this $85k to play blackjack, that it was only a matter of time until it was all gone. And the look he had in his eye, I think he thought the same.

I put up a fight for about 12 hours. I drank, I dined, I flirted and I did what I did best, I gambled with passion. I forgot about all of the negatives and I just did what I could to keep my love for the game of gambling alive for as long as it could last. My final hand was poetic. It almost beat the odds and seemed out of the ordinary. It was definitely quite the charming way to end a man's career thinking that he never did anything wrong. I had $40k left on the head. I bet $10k on a hand and was dealt two 7s against the dealer's 4. I decided to split them and put out another $10k. She gave me the first card and it was another 7, so I threw $10k more out there. So there I was in the middle of Vegas with three lucky sevens spread out in front of me and I only had $10k left to my name that lay shuffling between my fingers. She gave me an ace on the first seven giving me 18, a king on the second giving me 17 and the last seven she peeled off a four, giving me an 11. So I decided to double down and she gave me a 9 for a 20. Not too bad of a spread.

She took her time for whatever reason and the slower she went, the worse I felt. She turned over the card that was under the four and it was a six. It was the only card in the deck that I truly didn't want to see. Because I knew what the next card was going to be. Just like that, all of my Vegas memories kind of flashed before my eyes. And before she could take the card out from the shuffler I began to stand up. I had seen this scenario too many times in my life and I knew what was to come.

Very calmly and quietly she pulled out the ace of spades and put it down to the felt, she had made 21.

I watched my remaining $40k become Bellagio's property and I got up and walked away. I didn't feel anything and that was the problem. I had just watched my entire life be taken away from me and I had no one to blame but myself. I could have cut myself off when I had $1.7 million just a few months prior. Bought a house, put some away for stocks, invest it or actually listened to the hundreds of people that had tried to help me out along the way. But I didn't. I never wanted to listen to anyone's suggestions. The money had become my ammo for my addiction and I didn't want anything to get in the way of that. I was about to pay for it now I guess. I walked over to the bar and bought a long island and took a shot of patron.

I woke up to the feeling of something heavy poking me on my shoulder. I was sweating and I couldn't really feel my neck. First thing I thought was that I was in jail for some reason. When I finally turned over and felt the Vegas heat, it was three Las Vegas Policemen. I had fallen asleep on a bench a few hundred feet from the Bellagio front door and looked homeless given the beard. They asked where I was coming from and why I was passed out. I told them I was staying here at Bellagio and showed them my room key for confirmation. They asked for me to head up to my room before they arrested me for public intoxication since I smelled like a liquor store. They made sure that I got up and started to make my way towards the lobby.

As I walked in, I went to look down to see what time it was and my watch was gone. I checked my pockets but it was nowhere to be found. My guess is that someone walked past me in the middle of the night and stole it from me with no problems since I was in a coma. The cops mentioned that it took them a couple of minutes to wake me up. I had plans on pawning it in that day for at least $5k so I had some money to live on for a while. That was definitely a disheartening few seconds to take in.

I finally made it back to my room and I didn't have any options left. My phone was gone as well, but I still had my wallet and about a hundred bucks in cash left. I picked up the phone in my room and called my mother. She answered frantically.

"Mom, bring me home."

I hung up, but she knew what I meant. She bought my plane ticket for me and I left Vegas that night.

It was time for me to start over.

"Some people you meet in life and they stay with you for a period of time. Others become your brothers forever."

The Crew-

My father made certain that I was on some sort of sports team pretty much my entire life leading up to when I stopped playing baseball in college. I played throughout the full calendar year in every sport except football. There was something vital for a young man's life to be part of a group like that. To be amongst his peers that he would be going to school with, to cultivate that friendship and learn to grow up with each other. That camaraderie was an important life tool to learn as to what it was like to be part of a team. I lost all of that when I started to play cards. It's such a discrete lifestyle and profession that there isn't any type of teamwork when you're sitting there at the poker table manufacturing your own decisions that can costs you thousands upon thousands of dollars all on your own. It was always pleasant to have friends that are on the road doing the same thing. But it was pretty much just you and your conscious out there making life decisions.

When the plane touched down in Chicago, I had $56 in my pocket. That was it. Luckily the limo ride to the airport was free, so that saved me some cash, not that it really mattered anymore. I had a buddy of mine pick me up from Midway and he brought me home. My mother was in tears and open arms when I pulled into the driveway. I clipped and shaved the beard off before I left Vegas, but I still didn't look healthy. October was on the rise and the temperatures were finally dropping. It was nice actually to not have such immense heat painting your skin any time you were outside. My bags were hefty and full of filthy clothes. And I didn't have a clue as to what to do with my life now.

I gave her the complete rundown of as much material as I could without making her fear anymore about me. Even though I was home safe, she was still concerned about my well-being. My father was happy as well, but I could tell that he was disappointed in me and my actions. He was just always that kind of guy. Not that he wouldn't have been there for me through the negatives, but he just wanted me to be positive in the end. Since he always had some type of cold heart to the gambling world, I could understand his frustration.

I didn't find it logical for me to try and go back to school. I had the mindset of a corrupt alcoholic gambler right now, not a student spending a lot of money for an education. I didn't have any type of resume to really find a job either. I could probably ask some very trustworthy people to borrow me some cash or I could start asking around if there were any dealing jobs available at all of the house games somewhere within the city limits. Or I could go back to the charity games. I knew that any games in the city would welcome me in with open arms given my status. So, I did just that. My drinking stayed constant though. I got hooked up with a couple of dealing gigs in the city during the week and then on the weekends I went back to the charity games also. Not the same charity I used to go to when I was a teenager. There was a new one that had established in the suburbs that was created by my old friends. Guys that I knew since I was 19 years old and understood the predicament I was in. I felt embarrassed because they all knew the stakes I had been playing and the name I had made for myself over the years. They said of course I can come back with no questions asked.

At least I had the ability to deal cards seven days a week if I wanted to. I could maybe make $1,500-$2k per week in cash. Obviously nothing in the price range of my weeks out in Vegas, but this was the greatest it was going to get for a while. I had bills to pay and I needed to keep up with some consistent cash flow.

My first day at the charity games I was actually nervous. It had been almost two years since I had dealt poker at all and I knew it was going to take me a couple of hours to get into a rhythm. The dealers were one thing that I was going to have to deal with, but so were the players, too. The poker community in Chicago was enormous, but word traveled reckless in that society. About anything really, so I was sure there was going to be a lot of confused people out there when they heard I was back in town and dealing cards. Safe to say that I wasn't looking forward to answering more questions than I figured were already going to be thrown at me. I stopped at a liquor store along the way and got a coke and five small shots of Bacardi. I mixed them up on the way there for something to calm me down.

My long-time friend Tommy was the floor manager and it was pleasant to have some type of relationship with these guys, so that I didn't feel like I was going into all of this blind. I knew how to deal cards like the greatest, but this was all still exhausting to me. The only decent things really that I could think of, was that I would be making some tolerable cash, I could still be around the game which would generate possibilities for me in the future and I could drink the entire day too.

The charity games were a transportable casino. The moving truck arrived an hour before each event to unload everything and left an hour after the event was finished when the material was reloaded. The tables were worn down and the chips looked of age, but the dealers were precise and some of them even had some talent.

It was this group of guys that brought me back to life and made me feel alive again. The previous couple of months that I had just spent in Vegas, aside from losing everything I had, was a long excursion of sorrow and misery. But I couldn't really see any of it until it was too late since I was exceedingly intoxicated every day. These guys were young and full of energy. Even though I was about to celebrate my 23rd birthday, Vegas definitely tacked on some age to my life. The grey hairs began to form and I was drained all the time. Even though I came out of the deal penniless, I had a remarkable amount of knowledge for the game, more than anyone else that I knew.

When word got out about who I was by the end of the first event I dealt at, the guys invited me out for a late night dinner afterwards. The events ran until 1am, so there was still some time for all of us to go out and share our stories from throughout the day's event. And that's just what we did. We would deal all day long, go out afterwards at a local 24 hour restaurant and just laugh our asses off. We would share hysterical stories or talk about hands from the event that we all knew the guy had played mistakenly. They would ask me questions about Vegas or seek confirmation on a rumor they may have recently overheard. These were some of the most amazing guys I had ever met. They were all hustlers to me. They dealt on the weekends to make $500-$600 and then they would grind it out during the week. Whether it be playing online or going to the casino, these guys were simply grinders. Some bet ponies, others ran their own house games or were bookies. Anything they could do to make a dollar. It was nice to see another side of the gambling world that I never had the chance of really seeing the last couple of years. My life had been encapsulated with a luxurious life filled with substances that were non-existent by this point. It also reminded me a lot of myself five years prior. When I was trying to do anything I could to make as much money as possible and becoming an aspiring poker player at the same time. Even the guys that were older than me would come to me for guidance. The younger guys always shot me that look of being panicky, so sometimes I would have to start up discussions with them first and then they would open themselves up to me about anything.

These guys became my brothers. I looked forward to being with them on the weekends. During the week I would sometimes deal at some house games in the city, but I began staying with some of them at their houses and playing online instead. There were weeks that were a bust where we lost, but other weeks where we attained thousands. I needed to keep some type of momentum going for my sanity and future. That's if I still had one in poker.

We did nothing but play tournaments. I would drink a fifth of whiskey a day and just sit on a laptop under a hoody and grind all day long. The worst part was that I thought I was making a lead way in my life and progress. I didn't know if I should revamp my life for comparison of what success meant or compare what I was doing now to what I used to do. It was still exceedingly difficult for me not to think about all of damaging things that were still very fresh to me.

I turned 23 years old in a local bar among a few of my high school friends. It was tough for me not to drink long islands. I wanted to feel drunk and it was grueling to admit the amount of tolerance I had for alcohol at that point in my life. Even being back around them made me feel like a failure. I never had more than $1k in cash on me during that time period. I knew what I had demolished, but I didn't really know how to fix it. Since I was dealing and I had to pay attention to how much I was making and spending to make sure my bills got paid on time, just pissed me off even more. Some nights I was alright and other times I wasn't. I apparently started talking in my sleep about awful things and I didn't want to believe my friends about the things I was saying when they told me that.

The New Year was just that, a new year. I wanted to feel motivated, but I just couldn't. I had just kind of gotten used to what I was doing and getting by after paying my bills. I knew I was better than this, but at the same time there was no way for me to get back into the same caliber of game that I was playing without a substantial loan from someone. I just didn't have the heart to ask someone for a $100,000 favor, if not more. I just kept on going on the path I was on and waited for a miracle.

I had some success online during the weeks when I wasn't dealing. Mucks and I had become best friends and he let me stay at his place during the week. It pretty much became my money is your money kind of relationship. He was my best friend of The Crew and for the first time in a long time I trusted someone again. He was a respectable player but played particularly tight for tournament poker. That's how he got his nickname Mucks, he was always folding his hands. I wish he would have opened up his horizons and he could have definitely been a successful poker player. He was good nonetheless. He prized PLO and he was a good looking kid with a noble approach on life. We were in two different places in our lives, but we managed to meet halfway on majority of things. I am sure that I taught him a lot and in return he helped me out in a lot of ways.

I had done alright here and there and even got 13th in an FTOPS event for $8k. Mixed in with some other things, all of a sudden I had $18k. With the 2009 WSOP coming up, I felt it only necessary to head back to Vegas just one last time. There were plenty of other tournaments going on in Vegas other than the WSOP with smaller buy-ins that I could go out there and focus on. I had the longest break of my Vegas career away from that fantasy land where I felt I was ready to take a chance again. Or so I thought. I could get free rooms the entire time I was there as well, so I didn't have to worry about hospitality.

I had $13k online and another $5k in cash that I was taking with me. It only took a matter of a phone call and I could make that money online a reality and into my pocket for 90 cents on the dollar. But still, I felt that if I played daily tournaments up to $500 in value and maybe made some phone calls to get staked in anything, I could make a run at this lifestyle again. Anything was possible, as always.

My flight for Vegas left on May 28th 2009, the day after my father's birthday. The eight months that I was back home meant everything to me. The guys geared me up and kind of got me ready for going back to Vegas. Since I was playing online a lot, I was consistently seeing a lot of hands still. Then on the weekends I was dealing and repetitively discussing hands with The Crew and other players alike. They did the best they could to keep me in the game and on my toes and I will always love them for that. I think all of them knew how much the game meant to me and in their own ways they did everything to help me out. It hurts today that I can't see them as much as I did. I was part of a team again. And as long as forever chooses to go, I know that we will always have each other's backs and respect.

Mucks was my best friend as I had already stated. He loved PLO and I definitely thought he had potential for the game. He is currently in real estate and has a good head on his shoulders and I wish him the best.

Pete the Greek was the funniest of them all. He always had his own thing going on somewhere else. He was on his phone more than I was usually. I never knew if he was selling drugs on the side or something else, but given the concentration I would stake him to this day. Such an awesome dude and we still chat.

Black Jeff was just that, black. He was the only African American of the group. But he was if anything the most down to earth, realistic and intelligent one. He knew the game and understood it in ways that some of these other guys didn't. He also became one of my closest friends and also gave his two cents in everything that I did, which I entirely appreciate. He moved to Texas with his girlfriend and I haven't spoken to him much since.

Alex Ice Haze was a realist. He was the best free styling rapper I had ever seen in my life. He could dish off anything that was on his mind into a rhyme and I was impressed every time anything came out of his mouth. At the same time, if you wanted to talk about something with someone he was it. He was a humanist and would take a moment out to have a drink with you if he could. A father of three, he now deals at a casino and he deserves every piece of happiness that he finds.

Tommy was our boss and he was in charge of the floor pretty much. He was the guy I had known since we were kids. He really was that big brother to me while I was home. I truly love this kid. He watched out for me whenever he could and did anything in his power to get me back on my feet. He eventually moved out of state after I left and I haven't seen him since. I miss him a lot. If by chance I randomly ran into him anywhere in the country, I would give him a huge hug and just enjoy the moment I have with him. He was a true brother.

Johnny One Eye or Butch as we called him, got into the middle of a bar fight a few years prior and lost his eye. So his nickname resembled that. Sometimes he would take his fake eye out and use it as a card protector, making everyone disgusted but laugh obnoxiously by the randomness at the same time. He always made for a good person to be around and had a sense of humor like no other. Johnny had a huge passion for the game and his friends that surrounded him. I spent plenty of nights sleeping on his couch in his basement when I was too drunk to drive home. He too was one of my closest friends and part of him always will be. In the midst of me writing this book, Johnny passed away from reasons that will remain private. It was an awful feeling to hear about his death and we each found our own ways of coping with it. We all came to each other's sides and it showed what true friends we really were through such a difficult time. I miss him to this day and will always remember him. This book is entirely in memory of him. I miss you Johnny. Always will, I promise. Keep being you and I will see you when I see you.

Nubs lost one of his fingers at an early age and he was never the smartest one of the group. Like the rest of us, he made mistakes in his past. I still loved him more than anything. He was always trying to find some way to stay busy and content at the same time. He now travels on the circuit as a poker dealer and he deserves to be successful along the way.

Little Kenny was always one of my favorites. He was the fastest dealer I knew, but mixed in with some bad life decisions he might've missed some opportunities. I haven't seen the kid in a long time. I had heard some rumors that he was being staked in some high stakes PLO games, but hadn't seen him in a couple of years. I hope he is alive and well somewhere out there.

Serb I had known for a long time. He knew me longer than any of them actually; back when I was 19 years old and trying to become a noticeable poker player. He was a guy of many wives as we used to put it, but definitely had the most knowledge for the game out of any of those guys. He and I could talk for hours, capacitated with laughs but at the same time constructed with plenty of logical explanations to reasons why some hands played out the way that they did. He still grinds on a daily basis all over the city.

Big Lou was the father of the bunch. A father of a few kids, he was a working man seven days a week. But he was entirely a big teddy bear and had an awesome heart and consideration for the people he cared about. He definitely is an awesome dude that I miss to this day.

Runner Joe was the character of the group. He was as white as you got, but thought he was born another race. He had plenty of knowledge for different games, but his stupidity to life killed it. Always had a good time with him and to this day he still can't beat me in Gin. I am sure he will say otherwise though. He's currently a dealer at a casino too.

Chuck Norris is the Messiah. To this day he is still my best friend. Mainly because he is the only guy that fully understands me and what I have been through. He took over the floor manager position once Tommy left. He's the guy that's kind of done it right. He works on the weekends and then plays the same cash games throughout the week, regardless of how substantial his bankroll is. He's one of the most honest guys I ever met in the poker world. But, an alcoholic like the ghosts of me, he and I have plenty of stories to share a drink over with if we ever had a few free hours. You can find him abolishing souls four days a week on the felt somewhere on Chicago's city limits.

These few guys gave me some equilibrium for a while at a time when I truly needed it. They definitely rebuilt some stability that I needed to discover again in order to keep me in the game of poker. I needed to see how rigid it was in the poker world and remember that everything I had been doing out in Vegas was simply a blessing. I had blinded myself with cash, mirages and lies for such a long time that I forgot about the steps to get to that. That there were so many guys out there wishing they were on that level. But they were struggling and working to get to that. It is by no means a simple industry because you are able to turn on your television and see guys playing for astronomical amounts of money. It is a life that will terminate you even when you're doing it correctly.

These guys all had that drive to become something in poker in their own separate ways if they wanted to. I can honestly say that they were some of the best players I have ever known. At the same time, I didn't want to decimate that either. I wanted them to stay motivated. That drive was definitely something I had lost along the way. I had become entirely too complacent and filled with such a routine of winning and losing that I drifted away from the reasons why I was successful out there. Poker made me believe that life was magical in ways that are so difficult to explain through words on a piece of paper. I had a passion and love for the game that I had lost along the way. The cruel misguidance of a luxurious life, filled with shit I never needed before, drifted me off that successful path I once had a steady pace on. But The Crew made me remember why I loved this game as much as I did. I got to see life on their level for a while and just how the game can still be fun. I needed that involvement and with that, it gave me peace. Peace with myself and peace with an already haunting past.

It was time for me to go back to Vegas after an eight month hiatus. I figured I had been gone long enough and with the WSOP just starting, what a better time to venture back to that city. So off I went again.

For the boys- I love you guys, all of you. I will never forget that we were The Crew. It was special and meant the world to me. You guys saved my life.

"Our greatest weakness will always lie in giving up. The most absolute way to succeed is to try just one more time."

792 Hours in Vegas-

This time around there wasn't a chauffeur. There was no foreign gentleman waiting for me at baggage claim holding up a white sign with my name on it. I had to find my own bags and make my way to the cab line. For the first time in a long time I had to wait in line like everyone else. But I understood that and I got that. There was no more Bellagio. I was getting set up across the road at Paris in a suite just as big as the ones I used to get across the street. But something about it wasn't the same. The gorgeous women had turned into old ladies and their husbands they had known since before I was born. Not to say old ladies aren't attractive. My mother is the most beautiful woman on the planet, but I think I trailed off topic here. I didn't get the same energy that I wanted. They fucked up my room service all the time and it just simply wasn't home to me anymore since it wasn't Bellagio. Just like anything else, I had to adjust. I was back in my element and I needed to do whatever it took to get back on my feet again. This was my life. And I didn't wait that long to proclaim my own justice.

I flew in late and Caesars had a nice little nightly tournament. There were usually always 160 players that would register. But since it was the weekend there were about 200 players. A quick flashback when I was in Chicago just eight hours before, I told myself I wasn't going to drink at all for as long as possible. I couldn't last past security check without breaking that promise. So by the time I hit that nightly tournament I didn't really know if my name was Nicholas or Nicole.

I walked into the final table as the chip leader somehow. It made me sick sometimes that I had played my best poker and acquired my best gambling abilities when I was wasted. But for all you sober people out there before you judge me, would you talk to the hottest guy or girl you have ever seen in a more comfortable state drunk or sober? Fuck you if you said sober. Every one of you probably said drunk, so don't judge me. Same flowed with this game. Sometimes you made your best decisions wasted.

I won it. I had been in Vegas less than ten hours for the first time in eight months and I won the first tournament I played hammered for $6,400. When I was walking out of Caesars about five in the morning, I drifted so much that I ended up at the bar by the sports book and ended up playing blackjack until about noon. I won another $3k and my first day back I was up almost $10k. Just like that.

I walked back to Paris as that usual sun hit my face and I felt like I was going back in time. But I stopped at another blackjack table before I could find the elevator up to my room. I would end up sitting there for another three hours and lost back $5k. Only positive of the day is that I won that tournament and I knew I still had it in me, that drive for the game that I thought I had lost. Whether I was wasted or not at that point, the game proved to still be inside of me. I was up $5k on the day and hit the pillow hard that night in my less than acceptable suite.

After being there for a week I wasn't doing that well, I was down to about $4k and just couldn't get anything going. I was betting sports, playing blackjack and playing poker. Playing poker was keeping me afloat really. I was playing $15/$30 and winning, but losing my ass in the rest. I was barely eating and was just entirely depressed. I felt like I was letting people down and I was tired of calling my parents in the early hours of the morning and getting upset. I needed more money. So, I did the ultimate worst thing I ever did in my career, I started borrowing from everyone. No one had a problem borrowing it to me after I gave them a brief bullshit two minute story as to why I needed it. How I had gone bust out here and all of my money was back in Chicago, was always the easiest one to use. Since it was during the World Series of Poker, everyone I knew in the poker world was out in Vegas. I borrowed in ranges from $2k-$60k and everything in between. It became one loan after the other like some sort of assembly line. Even if I had cash, I still asked others to borrow from so that I could have more cash. I finally became entirely obsessed with money, worse than I ever had before.

Three security officers escorted me out of the Wynn somewhere around four in the morning. I had spilled my drink twice on the blackjack table like some child at a birthday party. The first time it was just ice, but when I spilled an entire glass of merlot on the felt and told the dealer to go fuck himself, it took all of three minutes for me to be out on the street. I had about $8k as a bankroll, owed $75k at this point and was staying with a friend off the strip in Summerlin. He insisted that it might be a good idea for me to stay a few miles away from the strip for a while to see if it changed up my luck, but it didn't. In just three weeks, I lost $90k and went below zero and into debt for the first time in my life. I hopped in a cab and gave the guy the address and passed out in the backseat.

These were all new feelings to me. The thought of being a failure and not living up to the name I had grown and built from scratch was disturbing to me. Being in that town it just made me think of all of the good times constantly. I guess I should be using those as motivational thoughts to get me back on the right track, but I kept looking at them as depressing images because I wasn't in that condition anymore. $8k used to be a single blackjack bet to me, now it was everything I had to work with.

I needed a drink. I was staying with two other guys and my room faced the east. Which was awful because of the sunrise every morning. For whatever reason the air conditioning didn't work in my room and even with the shades closed, my room still got hot as hell during the day. The fan did its own justice I guess, but it was still exhausting living quarters.

I poured some vodka on the rocks and just laid there in my bed. My window now looked out at an in ground pool and the neighbor's ugly house. No more 30th floor views with music playing in the background. I had to stand up to look outside now. I couldn't ask to have a couch put next to my window next to the cathedral tall glass that stretched across the entire room anymore. Times had changed and I wasn't adjusting well since coming back out here. I took one final sip of my drink and tried to forget that the last three weeks ever happened.

I borrowed another $10k from my friend and another $3k from a buddy of mine back home and had about $20k to work with. It was a new day. I decided to take a shot at the $100/$200 game at Bellagio. I figured I needed to play poker as much as possible and I needed cash as fast as possible. Ideally playing blackjack would have been the fastest way, but I hadn't won in blackjack pretty much the entire trip. I had a legit four buy-ins for the $100/$200 game and it was the game that I was most comfortable in. There were also three games going at Bellagio, so I knew that there was going to be plenty of action for a substantial amount of time.

It felt good to be back where all of it had begun. I mean, not my early career, but where Vegas became my second home. Because of that success, I had in that very room day in and day out, still gave me the courage to walk into that element with my head held high. It's like I watched myself grow up there.

I bought in for $5k and a couple of familiar faces asked where I had been. It was nice to see some of my old friends or acquaintances if you want to put it. Better yet, I just felt alright again. I was pleased all of a sudden and if anything I was anxious to see how this session was going to end up.

14 hours later and only a few long islands deep, I had my feet up on the chair next to me and we were playing four handed $200/$400. I was up $29k. Things were going good for me and my strongest game on this planet was short-handed high stakes limit hold-em. I had zero plans on getting up any time soon and was hoping that more players would show up. Another three hours went by and I and some random Asian guy had been playing heads up for a little while when he decided to call it a night. I won $36k and all of a sudden I had $55k. I was ecstatic and happy. On top of that, I was exhausted which was diverting me from walking over to the blackjack tables right now to keep on gambling since the game broke. I couldn't wait to come back after I got some rest and do it all over again.

I was dealt two 9s and she was showing a 3. I had $4k out there somehow on one bet and decided to split them. I got an 8 for one and made 17 and a king on the other for 19. She pulled out a 7 and a jack to make 20 and there went another $8k from my possession. The only game that I found worthy

of playing was the $100/$200 game and the list had
four people in front of me. I guess I had no other
decision than to play blackjack while I waited for an
open seat. I almost paid the floor man $1k to put my
name at the top of the list because I knew that this
bullshit was going to happen. The worst part about
scenarios like this when you're losing, is that you
hit a point where you feel like you can't leave. That
you just have to win it back at that table or go bust.
I had lost back everything I earned the day before
playing $200/$400 and another $9k on top of it. I
only had $10k left and was betting $2k a hand. Was
just kind of at a fuck it point with this trip, my
career and life.

Also, I couldn't just go play poker now either. I had
completely destroyed any aspiration of playing the
highest stakes at Bellagio right now because of an
awful blackjack session tonight. I had $9k left and
decided to bet it all. I literally got dealt blackjack,
got paid out $13,500 and got the fuck out of there. I
figured that was too poetic of a moment not to run
away. I took my $30k plus loss and hit the streets. I
bought the most expensive long island I could find
and took a shot of patron and realized that I needed
to walk around to get my mind off of things.

It became real to me. The town never changed in
the entire time I had been coming there. It was still
the same kinds of tourists, same drinks and
restaurants. They were building casinos because of
people like me. But I wondered where all of them
were. There were tourists, coming and going. I
didn't really see anything out of the norm on this
walk around the strip. The usual drunks, the backed
up traffic and the scorching heat that I had seem to
ignore all of the time. The heat never bothered me

really. It felt good most of the time to be honest. I
ended up at the Palazzo which is by far one of the
most gorgeous casinos in all of Vegas. I don't know
if it's the 200 foot ceilings or the women, but it just
makes you feel rich even when you're broke.

This is where it all ended.

Three more long islands deep I figured what a better
time than to play blackjack again. I had $23k and
bought in for about half of it. I was at a high stakes
table and betting $200 a hand on average for about
five hours. I was down $3k, nothing to really brag
about to be honest back in the old days. But given
my distress and the fact that I hadn't won in a
month at this game, I found it to be a good time to
finally book a score. So I went out of my element
and just started betting out of my means. Given my
predicament and what I owed, it probably wasn't
the best decision I ever made. I found that being
drunk was never an excuse anymore. There hadn't
been too many days in the last four years that I was
sober. It was just another day to me really.

I had $1800 left and decided to put it all on one
final bet. I was fed up, tired, wasted, hated this city
and didn't see what the difference was if I bet this
amount or the minimum by this point. Unless I went
on some ridiculous run sometime soon, this money
would be gone anyways. I was dealt a natural 20
against a jack. Fittingly and symbolically she turned
over an ace for blackjack.

I had $180 in my pocket and I was finished with
this town. I was a gentleman for once and told the
dealer to have a good night and walked out as quiet
as a mouse. It was an easy cab ride, just about 15

minutes back to the house. But I stayed awake this time. I stared out the window and wondered what the hell had just happened the last month or even to my life. The ambition and drive I had, had been destroyed from a run of bad luck and bad decisions that I could never overcome. Like I said, I never really had a sober decision in the gambling world. I woke up on planes blacked out asking the stewardess where we were heading with a drink in my hand. I told bouncers three times my size to fuck off and I had the balls to ask the best player of all time if he wanted to play heads up. The whiskey was more overwhelming in my own system than the fear and the blood flowing through my veins.

The cab dropped me off and I didn't really know what to do. It was about midnight and it was honestly a perfect night. I walked into a dark house and everyone was asleep. They had friends in from out of town and I think they had literally partied for about 36 hours straight. I wouldn't be surprised if they were all passed out.

I sat at the kitchen table without any of the lights turned on and made myself a gin and tonic. I just sat there and thought about everything like usual. I missed Eric. I missed Mindy. I missed the private jets and the type of attention I used to get from the public and people in Vegas. Most importantly, I missed just playing poker every day. For fun with my friends or where I did it best. Part of me was convinced I wasn't going to get that chance ever again. It gave me a true outlook on things. When you don't have money, you're nothing in this town. Or at least that's the way it felt since I had previously received the highest amount of attention throughout my unfortunate career.

I poured another drink and opened up the screen door and onto the pool area. I laid down on one of the beach chairs and just looked up at the sky. I found the moon and it was amazing to me. There I was, decapitating myself from my one dream and staring up in the sky at a dream I had wanted since I was a kid. The moon and space and being a pilot. Part of me felt like I was being mocked. I was probably wrong, but I still had so many fucked up thoughts running through my head that nothing really made sense at the moment.

When it was all said and done that night, I owed $163,000 spread out amongst 17 guys. Thankfully none of them were pissed off yet since all of them were millionaires pretty much. But I sat there poolside completely disgusted with myself. In a million different ways, but all of those ways pretty much came back to just a handful of reasons. We should all know what those are by this point. I wanted to go home. I wish I could say that I wanted my old life back but there was no chance in that happening. I was simply at an awful place in my life and I didn't know what to do. I had zero cash remaining; I owed the world and the alcohol had finally acquired a voice of its own.

So, I went for a drive.

"Life is a succession of lessons and experiences that must be lived in order to be understood and appreciated."

Fort Knox-

Laying on top of that car, I found myself staring off into space and feeling a few gusts of wind hit me. I made an attempt to count the stars that painted the sky with my finger pointing up in the air for guidance. I think I actually made it up to 150 or so before I gave up. The view was miserable but impeccable. Being 65 miles outside of Vegas and away from the bright lights, gave me a chance to see the beauty that life held just above the earth that made me wonder how life could get this exhausting and sad.

The sight was something I had never experienced before. Like I said in the beginning of all of this, my ultimate life dream as a kid was to be an astronaut. Not just by thought or on a whim either, but I wanted to be able to rocket into outer space with no worries behind me. I wanted to know what it would be like to go thousands of miles per hour and leave my troubles behind me back on earth. And right now, I was just that, I was an astronaut out here. I had just lived a fast paced life that had me going a million miles per hour constantly for what felt like an eternity. Here and there and this and that. All in a while mixed in with every living possible piece of bullshit you could ever think of. It was powerful and sad, but sexy in all of its ways. Then all of a sudden that journey I was living brought me here. Out here in the middle of nowhere staring up at the most beautiful sight I had ever seen in my life. If you can imagine being in the middle of the desert on a perfect summer night, how many stars do you think are visible? Every fucking one that is out there, literally. And it was the best moment of my life. I had become an astronaut right there in that moment. I had become synced in the moment from staring off at so many random different designs the sky had to offer me. Being on top of the car, I truly felt like I was just floating in outer space glaring off into the galaxy. It was just one of those moments in life you never forget and you try and cherish the best that you can. Those few seconds of clarity diverted my mind from the real reason why I drove all the way out here in the middle of the night. But it wasn't enough.

I took a sip from the bottle of gin and began to cry. I didn't know how I got to this point. I could see myself smiling on those private jets. Or the conversation I had with that gorgeous stewardess on that flight back to Vegas. I missed the pineapple drink the waitresses used to make me at the Skyscraper game. It pissed me off that I couldn't remember the names of the two girls Eric and I were hitting on at the Cubs game just a few days before he died. I wished that I got to know the names of the people at the Southwest Airlines counter that I saw so many times a week. I missed my boys back home and spoiling them with anything they ever wanted. That image of Mindy with that other guy made me want to roll over and throw up, but I still missed her more than anything.

I had been alone so many times the last few years, but this wasn't a feeling of being alone right now. This was a feeling of emptiness. There was no hope left. There was no fixing the problem anymore. I loved life more than life itself, but I didn't know how to live life anymore if I couldn't keep up with the ways I had been used to and made a life out of. I had to finally face the consequences.

This time around I took a long sip of that gin that sat next to me like it was my only friend. The 9mm pistol rested quietly on my chest with one bullet in the chamber. Assuming from all of the movies I had seen in my lifetime, that's all it would take to end these thoughts once and for all. It was the most dangerous thing in the world right now and it just sat there a few inches below my chin like it was my best friend. Like it knew that it was doing me a favor. I hadn't fired a gun since I was a kid at a shooting range, but I figured it didn't take much talent to put a gun to your head and pull a trigger either. I didn't know if I should put it under my chin or next to my brain. I remembered hearing awful stories of guys putting it under their chin, pulling the trigger and missing their brain and surviving. I don't think it can get much worse than that. So I made the decision to put it just above my right ear.

Staring at the stars, I picked up the gun and put it next to my head with my finger on the trigger and I waited. I waited to die or I waited for a miracle to convince me to live.

71 fish we caught that day, I think. For whatever reason that was the first thing I thought of when that cold piece of steel touched the side of my head. I couldn't have been more than nine years old when my father and I set up shop underneath a random bridge somewhere on some perfect summer day. We caught 65 bluegills and a handful of other fish. It was my thing to keep all of them in a single bucket until it was too capacitated and my father would tell me I had to dump them back into the river. He said that we could fish all day and at the end of the day I had to bring the biggest one home with me. I did and for whatever reason I saw it necessary to name him George. He actually survived for about another six years in a fish tank I had in my house. But we didn't care about the size of the fish. I wish I knew then why my father took me there that day. And what he was thinking. We were best pals, have been forever. 98% of the reason I want to be a father so bad is because my dad has been my best friend since the day I was born. That's a once in a lifetime relationship.

Ten more minutes had passed and my arm was still raised and the gun was still flushed with my skin. I had made a million life changing decisions in the

last few years, but this came to be the hardest. I
guess I didn't see a point of living anymore. I felt
that I had let down everyone I knew. I didn't have
the energy to lose anymore and I didn't want to lose
anymore. I hated it. No one likes to lose. Let alone
at a magnitude such as the levels I was gambling at.
So I said fuck it. The last words I ever said were the
only words I wanted to say.

"Love you Mom and Dad."

I had one last sip of the gin, took a deep breath and
pulled the trigger.

Safety.

My inexperience to that of infantry and guns and
everything that came along with it, made me forget
to remove the safety. A simple few seconds of
silence in the middle of the desert was all I heard.
And it was all that I needed. I sat up right away like
I was waking up from a bad dream. I was sweating
profusely and couldn't believe what had just
happened. Like black and white, or an on and off
switch, I slid back down off the car, emptied the
chamber and threw the gun as far as I could into the
desert. I was reborn.

I kept the bullet and it rested innocently and silently
in my pocket. When I made it back to the house, I
emailed my mother and I told her I loved her. I gave
her a déjà vu moment and told her to bring me
home once and for all. She bought my plane ticket
home again and couldn't be happier.

I went downstairs and back outside by the pool area
and watched the sun come up. All of those stars that

had just watched over me were disappearing one by one as the daylight took over. I was still speechless.

I started to pack up my shit and knew it was time to call it quits with this lifestyle. I told my friends that I was staying with that I may see them sometime soon but I knew that wasn't going to happen. The one buddy of mine drove to me the airport. I asked him if we could stop at Bellagio on the way to McCarren Airport. We threw my shit into the car I had just been in a few hours before and headed towards the strip.

My flight was supposed to be somewhere around 6pm, so I assumed it was just early afternoon. Mikey had a new shift where he was working around that timeframe. My buddy dropped me off in the front driveway and waited for me and I ran inside hoping he would be there. When I ran up to the high stakes area, he was on the phone and gave me the one second signal with his finger. Like I said before, he was like my mentor in Vegas. If anything, he had spent more time watching over me than anyone else. Like a guardian. He admitted to me once that he would stay an extra hour or two outside of his work schedule to make sure that I was happy and everything was alright and that I had the correct security. He got off the phone and he saw that I was in a hurry.

"I need a favor, Mikey. Run my player card and see what security box number is mine."

I pulled an envelope out of my pocket that contained the bullet that never fired.

"I need you to make sure that this makes it to that box, no questions asked. And that it stays there forever. I know that I have enough comps in this hotel where I could stay here for free for years. So let's just call it an even trade and make sure that this gets put there and never opens up ever again."

He said of course and I hugged him and cried. I told him thank you again a few times, turned around and headed back to the lobby and out the front door.

The bullet was going to be transported into another set of security boxes that stayed in the Bellagio vault four stories below the Earth. And it'll stay there forever. It was my most prized possession and more valuable to me than anything else in the world.

It became my own Fort Knox.

I walked in to the airport for the last time and I felt like I had been resurrected. I couldn't wait to get home and start a new life. I had no idea as to what I was going to do though. I was going to have to take my life and do a complete 180. It was going to be a process that was going to have to be renewed every single day in order to make me better. I wanted to be a better person, but I had to acquire new hobbies and interests too. More importantly, my drinking was going to have to be cut down to a minimum somehow for any of that to happen.

I had been out here for 33 days straight. I was on the go every single second and drinking every minute of it. Even as I made my way down to the end of the long walk to the Southwest terminal, I had a drink in my hand. Throughout the last few weeks, I had said a handful of times that I wished it would rain in this town. I must have said it at least eight or nine times in random conversations. Anything to change up the element of this city could be a nice change of pace for me. Weather can affect so many people and make them do different things. As I was standing there at the window and looking out at the strip, fittingly and symbolically, a single rain drop hit the window directly in front of me. It was such a moment. And with only a few clouds in the sky, it began to rain over the airport for only about three minutes and then it was gone. I don't know, I felt like it was Eric. I felt like it was a signal to some degree that he was there with me and I began to cry. There were just certain emotions that I couldn't really control anymore. Knowing that me being alive from what happened the night before, may have had something to do with him.

"Travelers, your flight to Chicago-Midway is now boarding."

"I'll love you until the end."

December & 73 Reasons-

Love. It comes in all shapes and sizes. It's that one thing in life that has a billion different definitions because it is unique in everyone's own individual ways. It can do the craziest of things to your mind, body and a thousand other walks of life. In return, it's an important factor in life. I know that there are some people out there that it just isn't for them. They either never want to get married or never want to have kids. And that's fine, to each their own. For me though, it's definitely something I want to share with someone eventually. Those are just the special things in life, things that they can't teach you in a classroom or by reading about it in a book. You just have to wake up and learn how to live within it on your own. You have to discover it on your own and understand that it is definitely one of life's biggest mysteries.

I had been home for about five months by this point and a buddy of mine that owed me some cash, roughly $800 said I could come to the city and pick it up if I wanted to. Every dollar counted at this point. I was paying people back any time I had cash, but at the same time I still had about $15k out there that I was trying to collect from guys that owed me too. I was an idiot sometimes though. Gambling was still highly in my blood and sometimes I ventured off to the casino and would blow it all playing blackjack. But I was convincing myself that I was getting healthier. Mentally, physically, just everything really.

He lived in Bucktown and I hadn't seen him for a while. So we had a little while to catch up, exchanged the cash and I left. Down the street from his place was a little bar and I was starving and could always go for a drink. It was cold being the beginning of December, so I took the two minute stroll on down. It was just a small place with a handful of tables and a long bar. Looked kind of old, but the Bulls were playing and I had nothing else to do.

I sat at the end of the bar a few chairs away from a couple that you could tell was just in love. They sat facing towards each other and were splitting an appetizer. Full of laughs and touching, they just looked happy. After I got my burger and ordered my second drink, in walked a brunette that I had to do a double take on because of how beautiful she was. I was waiting for a guy or another girl to walk in behind her, but she came in alone. She overshot all of the available chairs at the bar between the door and the cute couple and sat directly to my right but a chair away. What the fuck was happening?

Nervous enough, I tried not to get caught looking at her. She was perfect. Maybe 5'3, her neck was covered with a dark blue scarf, she was wearing a long grey winter coat and she had a smile that I still remember to this day. She took all of it off when she sat down though and I tried to act as if I had never seen her come in to begin with. She had on tall boots, dark jeans and a skin tight white sweater.

Ten minutes went by and she had been sipping on a martini when her lovely voice caught me completely off guard as she started up a conversation with me.

"Sometimes you just need to find that much needed drink, right?" She said.

It began a conversation that would last the next nine hours. Within no time she moved over a chair and we became this couple that was now facing each other and full of laughs and happiness. Truly felt like I had known this girl my entire life. We ordered nachos, took shots and kept drinking. The best part was just the in depth conversation that never seemed to have a moment of silence. It had been a long time since I had been on a date or with a woman, but I couldn't figure out what this was really. It was my own few hours of spontaneous connection mixed in with some serendipity.

We talked about everything. She was a student at DePaul and finishing up her last semester. She was originally from Wisconsin, but her family now lived in Kentucky. Because of that, she had a small southern accent which made her even sexier. She wasn't sure if she would move back south to live with her family after this semester was over with. Or stay in Chicago and try to start a new life here. She was smart and witty, but made eye contact the entire time and listened to everything I was saying. Communication is so important in this world and definitely a quality I hope to find in a woman someday. I told her all about Vegas and she was just fascinated. Everything was still very recent to me, so it was fresh off my mind to explain in great detail. She didn't look down on me for not having a college education, rather, she was entirely amazed by the things I had been through and was full of questions too.

The bartender let us know that it was last call. I decided to order a martini like the ones she had been drinking just to get a taste. We talked for a few more minutes and made our way out the door. Right there on the freezing sidewalk just outside the bar, she invited me back to her place which was coincidentally just around the block. I couldn't refuse and took her up on her offer.

She had a cute little apartment all on her own. Surrounded with brick walls and hardwood floors, it was comfortable and cozy given the temperature outside the window. She made us a couple of drinks and we sat close on her couch and kept on talking. We talked about relationships and experiences, sex and traveling. Just anything you could think of really. A couple of hours had gone by and it was probably time for me to go. The sun was coming up soon and I didn't feel like drinking anymore.

"Well, you have two options here sir. You can either take me to my room to have sex with me for the remainder of the morning, we exchange numbers, find each other on Facebook, maybe see each other again or even date for a while. Then maybe something stupid happens a year from now and we break up and we hate each other forever."

So I asked her what the second option is.

"I walk you to the door and you leave and I never see you again. But before you leave we kiss for at least five minutes of passionate kissing. We never exchange phone numbers, we never find each other on Facebook and we still don't tell each other our names. And we remember each other forever because this was one of the best nights of my life."

That was special to me, because she was right. Through the midst of everything happening to me as of recently and coming back to Chicago alive, she was a breath of fresh air. A few hours of peace from the demons of my past and a discovered hidden love that could have never happened if I went one way that night and she went the other. We found each other for a few hours and it was one of the most meaningful nights of my life.

I helped her clean up our drinks and folded up the blanket we had over our legs. It was one of the most difficult decisions I ever made but I started my way towards her door to leave. I turned around, grabbed both of her cheeks as gently as possible and we kissed for about ten minutes. It was perfect. I hugged her tightly and said thanks and kissed her on her forehead one more time and walked out. She stood in the doorway as I walked down the stairs and the last thing she ever said to me started some type of inspiration that is clearly now an accomplishment.

"Do me a favor and write a book about all of your gambling experiences. It may change your life. I know that I would read it."

She was right, again. Maybe putting all of it on paper would help me find peace with my past. To just get the story out there once and for all, maybe it could inspire people. Maybe it could be an inspiration to not only gamblers that anything is possible, but just anybody that could relate to it all. That if you put in the work ethic, there's no reason to think about fear. It doesn't exist if you know that you are confident in what it is that you are doing and passionate about in life.

Over the course of time and as I moved forward in life, I went both ways about that night with her. Sometimes I was upset we didn't see each other ever again and other times I wasn't. I genuinely understood how exceptional and meaningful those few hours were to the both of us. It was just one of those moments in life that I was going to treasure forever.

I have thought about the thousands of people that I have come in contact with in the last four years since that night towards the end of 2009, and I have forgotten about all of them for the most part. But I still remember everything about her. The way she smelled and how she laughed. Or how we only kissed for a few minutes, but it felt like it went on for hours. How I hate myself a little more every day for not trying to somehow find her after that night. But how I love the fact that I will always have that night and those few hours locked away inside my heart one way or the other forever.

I named her December.

Three years passed and I had been dating some here and there but couldn't get anything going. I met Marie in 2012 and my life was finally coming together and changing for the better. She made me happier than any girl I had ever been with in my entire life. I blame a lot of that on maturity I think. The more I progressed in life and took care of my debt which was about gone; the more I began to appreciate things I had never thought of before. This in return, opened up doors for me and sights I had never seen or experienced either. Which would end up creating a whole new path to live. The way I fell in love with her was different than that of Mindy. I blame it on age and life experiences to be honest. Things were clearer for me as another day went by in my new life. I looked at things differently and was on a positive path.

The two of us had a perfect relationship. I mean that. I understand that nothing is perfect in this life, but it worried me sometimes that I couldn't find anything wrong with her or us in general. We never fought about anything, supported each other entirely, had great sex and we loved each other's families. I was at an age and a time in my life where everyone around me was getting married and having families. Even though we weren't at that point yet to experience that by any means, by default I started to naturally see her in those roles somewhere down the road in our future. Given that, it made me fall very in love with her rather quickly. I couldn't help myself.

She did everything right, was loveable in all ways and I adored her to death. I was obsessed with her smile and I treasured that every day that I saw her, I discovered new reasons to fall in love with her all over again. She was overwhelming on so many different walks of life and it was peaceful how comfortable we were together. Sometimes we would finish each other's sentences and other times we would do anything that we could to annoy each other. The best part about us was that she was my best friend. We had acquired both relationships along the way. Which made everything about us being together more meaningful.

I was lying in bed one night and Marie and I were texting each other. I told her that I wished she was here next to me for 73 different reasons. She told me to name 2 of them and I came back with all 73, kind of. I legitimately named off 22 reasons one by one in a single text and then for number 23-73 I put "to fall in love with you more and more each day." But she still loved it and appreciated it since I could name off 23 reasons that quickly and spontaneously.

Time moved on, then without any warning, she decided to break things off with us and I was devastated. I tried my best to understand or figure out why, but even she couldn't give me an explanation. Not to go back in time or anything, but sometimes love just ain't enough. And I get that. Our problem was that we were never friends before knowing each other. We just jumped into getting to know one another to primarily find a relationship. So us trying to continue on to be friends, most likely wasn't going to happen. There was too much love there for me. Then when you tack on developing emotions of losing her, I knew it wouldn't work out.

She was as confused as I was, if not more. We had this faultless relationship, but in the end something was missing for her. I didn't have the heart to fight with her because I was still too madly in love with her and I didn't want to add to the hurt by starting irrelevant arguments. The conversations went back and forth for a while. More of me trying to convince her that we should stay together. Since I couldn't find anything out of place and she still couldn't figure out why this was happening. She was sincere and honest and she never ignored any of my questions. She said that she didn't think that she could love me at the same level as I treated her and degree that I loved her. It was just an unfortunate situation that I'll never be able to understand in the end.

I tried to convince myself that I would wake up one morning to eight text messages or three missed calls and it would be her telling me she wants me back. Hopefully that she just had to figure some things out for herself. I stared at my phone all the time because I never ended up getting that from her. My drinking resurfaced itself for a solid two months straight after the breakup, every night. Not just a few beers either. I was drinking two bottles of wine a night usually or twelve beers at least. I wanted to do anything I could to just feel numb about the situation. Even if that meant that it was only going to be for just a couple of hours. I just didn't know how else to handle these feelings and emotions that I didn't think I would've ever gotten from her.

I couldn't stand checking in on her anymore, so I wrote her a long goodbye message and deleted her from Facebook. I understand it's pathetic, but we all know it can be an easy way to keep tabs on someone. I was tired of doing it a hundred times a day and that was that really. I felt that out of respect for her, I didn't want to become more obsessive than I already was. Especially since it was becoming clearer that we were never going to be us again.

But before I deleted her from my life, or attempted to, I tried one last way to convince her to come back to me. I had taken a screenshot that night when I told her reasons 1-23 of why I loved her and remembered that I left out the exact reasons for 23-73. So, with a bottle of wine in my system, I filled in all of the remaining 50 reasons. The reasons that I loved her just came to me naturally and it only took me a few minutes to finish. I promised her I would and I did and I sent it to her. I hoped that maybe that would shed some light on her heart and give us another chance at making each other happy.

Unfortunately, it didn't work. She never changed her mind and I had no other choice than to respect that. Learning to live again all alone and single was a whole new life. I had to remember how to do things again without her presence and on my own. I had to stop staring at my phone and neglecting the urgency to text her to tell her how beautiful she was every morning. Which I made sure that I did every single day when we were together. The same routines had to end or I was never going to get better. They played out like they always had for a while and then eventually died out. But every morning since, I've picked up my phone to text her and tell her I miss her. But I always forget to hit send. I think about her all the time. My mind has tried to erase her from my life, but clearly it never will. I guess if I can give a girl 73 legit reasons as to why I love her more than anything in the world and still not make her change her mind that it just wasn't meant to be.

I don't blame Marie for her decision. The concept of two humans conjoining their lives together forever is entirely exhausting to even think about. But it's well worth the fight in my book. I understand that we all have our own lives and we all have to trust ourselves more than anyone. Our thoughts and our decisions are going to reflect how our lives end up in the end. Just because I saw Marie to be the one for me, doesn't mean that I was the one for her. That's why to me, love is just some never ending mystery, always will be too. Even when I'm eventually married to the love of my life and we are picking out names for our children, it will always be a mystery. You have to find new ways to make that person happy every day. You have to rediscover each other every morning you wake up to make sure that the ending is told just right. It's such a long journey for the couples that do it correctly. But it's by far the most beautiful journey of them all at the same time.

I tell you about these two women because the day after I left December in 2009, I started to write this book. But I had to stop at certain points and probably made the attempt over twenty times to get it going. I couldn't get in the flow or maybe I couldn't figure out what to write. My grammar wasn't the greatest back then and I just couldn't find that inner voice that I wanted the reader to be able to hear. Everything was still too fresh on my mind and I found myself getting emotional more often than being able to write a meaningful story. I had plenty of people when I was living my poker career, tell me that my life would be one hell of a movie. But December was the first one to ever tell me to write a book about it. Even though all of those rough drafts and attempts are long gone and have since been deleted, it gave me plenty of ideas if I ever did write a book, as to the direction I would want the story to be told. That initiation was definitely important to this accomplishment.

As for Marie, just three days after she ended things, was when I started the beginning of what you've been holding. I felt compelled to get all of this out of my heart and into the world once and for all. I needed something to keep me busy and I figured it was the best time to do so. I was a mess when she called it quits and every day my mind was thinking of ways I could tell this story a little bit better. Anything to keep me the least bit distracted from the feelings that could leave me in tears if I wasn't careful enough at any given second. I also felt that all of those new mixed emotions I was experiencing could help me write a more significant story. Since now I pretty much knew that it was for a better purpose.

Unfortunately, we don't talk anymore and it hurts. It kills me because up to this point in my life as I type this, she's been the most meaningful person for it, whether she's a part of it or not. I can still hear her laugh and I remember all of her mannerisms. The ones that she thought annoyed me were actually the ones that I loved the most. I miss throwing away her trash after a meal and waking up next to her innocent self. She was perfect.

I by no means was ready to lose her as fast as I did. I thought the pain that I felt from my poker career was gone, but the emptiness and confusion that she casted upon me with no warning was another experience that I had to hit head on. I still find myself thinking about her and the comforting thoughts of what it may have been like. It's not because I can't see her anymore and it's not because we can't argue over where to go dinner either. It's because I lost two people that day when she parted our ways for us. I lost my girlfriend and I lost my best friend. But I will never have a bad thing to say about her. She was special. In a million ways and I've only explained a handful of them.

Life will go on, always does and it has. Even when I'm married, part of me will always think about Marie. Where she might be and if she's happy, or if she's annoyed by some random shit or being a smartass. Basically all of the superlatives that made me fall in love with her from the start.

Marie was the ultimate inspiration for this book. None of this would have been completed without the motivation I found from our breakup. I will always have this to thank her for. It will be a lifelong gift that I will always be able to have with me.

I love December in a different way than I love Marie. I could probably try and explain it, but it's just that special to me that I would rather keep it to myself for once. They're the only two women up to this point in my life that I know I am always going to miss. And that I would do anything for if I was ever given the chance to again. They were both inspirations to me in their own ways and I will always thank them for that. They live now only within my memory. And if that's the only way that I can have them in my life, I've come to an understanding about that.

I've come to the conclusion that people are going to come in and out of your life forever. Every single day. In so many different shocking and life changing ways. It's truly up to you how you want to value the time that you spend with them to where you value the measures of what it just might mean.

Love is special. When you notice it or discover it, embrace it. Don't be afraid of it. And if you are, that's ok too. It's supposed to be scary and adventurous. It helps you grow and it helps you survive if you do it right. Even when it's perfect it may never make sense.

I know that I will always love both of them until the end.

"The only way to get the most out of life is to somehow someway look at it as an adventure."

New Life-

I was home and my Vegas days had come to an emotional end. It was hard to believe that five months had passed since that life changing night out there on top of that car in the middle of the desert. But it was the start to something new. When I came home, I went and lived with my father for about three months. He lives in a small country town 79 miles south of Chicago. It was exactly what I needed. I needed to just be isolated for a while from the outside world. I caught up on five years of lost sleep and did little things around the house to gain momentum for life again. I built a walkway for him made out of 119 pieces of stone, did various chores every day around the house, watched the dog and did the grocery shopping as well. Little things, but also important things to make me find some type of life balance.

Granted I still drank every day pretty much. The local bars were only a couple of blocks away. He had a girlfriend that lived an hour away, so he spent a majority of his time there since his office was only a few miles away from her place. I really just needed time to myself to figure out what I wanted to do now and what my next move was going to be. Internet poker was still around and I turned $200 into about $35k in winnings in the time I spent down there with him. I used $10k of it to start the process of paying back all of the money I owed to people. Every little bit counted I guess.

In October of 2009 I eventually moved back north to live with my mother and started to look for a job. I knew that I didn't have the energy just yet to go back to school, nor did I have the funds either. My next goal right now was to pay back everyone I owed. The remaining balance was just under $160,000 spread out amongst seventeen guys. Because I knew that there was never going to be a way for me to carry on with the rest of my life peacefully, until all of that was gone and taken care of. I started applying for jobs left and right. Anything from the local video store to being a waiter. Just anything at this point to start getting into a routine. I started going to the gym three or four times a week and was helping my mother with anything she needed around the house. It was time for me to start being a good person.

I got hired by Jewel and was working in the meat section. I was packaging and restocking that portion of the store and jumping in and out of ice cold freezers. I went from betting $125,000 on a single blackjack hand, to making $8.50 an hour. I was only there for about two weeks when I got a phone call that has changed my life forever. I responded to an ad online for data entry a few weeks before, it turned out to be for the railroad. They wanted to bring me in for an interview and a week later I got another call from the Director telling me I was miraculously hired.

I am still with them four years later once 2013 comes to a close. I work at the largest intermodal facility in the entire country. I love trains and everything about working at a rail yard. I have several tasks and there are thousands of people relying on me on a daily basis. Between clients, customers and close to a thousand trucking companies coming in and out of the yard, I have the ability every day to wake up and give life my all and make a difference to society. To change the world with every decision I make is such a gratifying thing to have. My days start when the sun has just come up and sometimes I don't leave the yard until the sun has disappeared. I can't express it enough how far I have come with the railroad. I would have never thought that this would be my life when I was being flown around on private jets just six years before. Life is going to keep on moving whether you are ready for it or not and you need to learn how to stay with it and keep up. The railroad saved my life.

I get reminded every day one way or the other about the life I once had. Those conversations have become easier as time passes, but they still bring me back to some of the lowest points in my life. Sometimes its young guys at the charity games asking me questions, or people I work with that know small bits and pieces about my past. Or when I used to go back to the casino and random people would spot me and know me but I didn't know them. Or I just didn't remember them. They always had a look on their face like they had seen a ghost. They would ask me questions about where I had been or exactly what happened to me. How they never thought I would have ever stopped playing cards. Or that they had heard stories along the way about me having a fall out. But never knew what story to believe.

Fittingly, I found my answer in 2012. After being away from the whole scene for about four years, I went to Harrah's in Joliet to play some blackjack or poker with a few hundred bucks. Knowing that I could win $5k and not even crack a smile, but I missed the game. I missed the game that made me feel alive and larger than life for years. I missed what it was like cutting chips, making moves and being noticed by the floor men because of the way I was handling my money and understood the game. That those few seconds of being noticed could cast a natural high over me where I didn't care if I lost the $400 in front of me or not. Because it made me feel like I was back in the high stakes pits at

Bellagio all over again with Mikey. But these guys didn't know about the player they were looking at. Or the things I had been through. To hold onto my identity, I refused to give my player's card to them after I came back from Vegas for good. That's all they had to do was make one phone call and they could pull up all of my stats and sessions at all Harrah's properties across the country since the day I was able to gamble. Like my $84k loss at Caesars or my $128k victory at the Rio and pretty much everything in between. For now, I just wanted to be left alone. In an element that I once controlled out on the west coast to the highest of magnitudes, I was alright with just blending in with the rest of the world from now on.

But I went this time to play poker on a weekend. The tables were packed and there was a list. Figured that while I was waiting I would walk to the bar and grab a V8 or a soda, sounds different but the same right? As I was waiting for my drink, a guy I kind of remembered was sitting at the bar playing video poker. He must have looked up and spotted me because he made it very clear that he remembered me. He told me a quick little story that night that made me leave the casino and I have never been back since.

"Nick?"

"Yes?" He didn't let me say a word until he was finished with everything he was about to tell me.

"I thought it was you, it looked like you, but I didn't want to believe it was you. I saw you over by the poker room and figured that if you were going to be playing that it wasn't smart for me to play at all. So now I sit here at this video poker machine drinking vodka and trying to make jacks or better for the remainder of my evening. You probably don't remember me. A long time ago you went to a game in the city up in the Hancock building called "The Skyscraper Game." Maybe you remember me now that I have mentioned it, but I was the dealer. I was only a kid back then, about 19. I just want to let you know now that I have the chance, to tell you that you inspired me to be a poker player. You did things that I had never seen before or understood. The way you carried yourself, the alcohol you drank. But just the way you won man. The cash, the loads of cash you would win. I never saw you lose. Did you ever lose? I wanted to be a pro for a living. But in the end I kind of realized how difficult it was by dealing the stakes I had the opportunity of dealing to you. But you changed my life. I always kind of hoped that I would see you again to tell you that. So that you knew that I felt that, for yourself. The game at Tyler's has since died, but it wasn't until a few years later that I moved on and started to deal at a new game out in the suburbs, that a random face walked in the room and started rambling about his past experiences in the city. He made me understand something about your legacy that night. He went on and on about the stakes he had played and the big names he had played with from the underground games. It was the first time he had ever been to the game and none of us knew him. He never mentioned a name but he went on and on about this kid he once knew. How he did everything right. How he dominated every game he ever went to and he was the best all-around poker player and dealer in Chicago. How he was on television and was if anything the greatest of all time. But, he was an alcoholic and it ruined him. It ruined his dreams. It ruined the path that so many people had supported him on. He became a degenerate gambler and somehow lost his love for poker. Then he looked me right in the face and said this to me in a very sentimental way, like you were possibly good friends once upon a time or something."

"But he's extraordinary, you want to know why? Because he's a myth, that's the easiest way to put it. He's a legend because you and I, two guys who don't even know each other are talking about him years later. He's the guy that all of us one way or the other want to be like. He's alive, somewhere out there. And to a few lucky guys he's still alive to the poker world, because we remember how he was. But he's a ghost to the rest of the poker scene. Chances are none of us will ever see him again. We will never know what he felt and we will never be able to understand the courage and self-confidence that an individual must have to do the things that he

did. And in the end be successful on top of it. He
was the greatest I ever played with."

After he was finally finished with his story I looked
him right in the face and I said the first thing that
came to my head.

"I have to admit, he sounds like one hell of a guy.
But, do you really think that the character you just
described would be the alcoholic at Joliet casino on
a weekend, ordering a V8 while waiting for a seat in
a $2/$5 No Limit game?"

He looked confused as shit, so I eventually laughed
and I told him thank you. It was a comforting story
and I said of course I remembered him. He was a
phenomenal poker dealer from what I could recall.
He was quick and accurate and had passion for what
he was doing given the stakes he was coordinating,
especially at such a young age. I shook his hand,
thanked him, walked a few feet to leave and turned
back around.

"Hey kid!"

I threw him the $500 chip that was in my pocket
that I was going to buy in with at the cash game I
was waiting for. Knowing that if I walked past a
blackjack table right now, I would just sit down
with it, my name would get rolled on the poker list,
I would lose it in no time and go home upset with
myself.

"Just do me a favor and hold on to that for as long as you can. Maybe someday you'll understand why. Good luck."

And I walked away before he could say anything.

All of it kind of happened in slow motion. I made my way towards the door with my hands in my pockets and my hat pulled down low. He kind of proved to me that night that I didn't need to gamble anymore in order to win. I'd already won. I lived a life that I built on my own from scratch. No plans or goals. I just kind of did it and said fuck it. Even though I came home broke and owed so much money to the world, I still succeeded in a million life changing ways. Ways that they can't teach you in school or by taking tests. And as another day comes and goes in this new beautiful life I have now, that captivating toxic vision I still have of who I was, disappears a little more and more each day. But clearly, it will always be with me. There isn't a day that goes by that I don't miss it though. Haven't you ever wanted to take a chance on something you were terrified of doing? Well, I highly suggest that you give it a shot. Experiencing life outside of your means and comfort zone is something that everyone should have the opportunity of experiencing one time or as many times as they want. Thankfully, the regrets have transformed themselves into joyful memories and the whiskey on my breath lies buried somewhere out there in the desert.

In the summer of 2013, the wheels below me touched down in Vegas for my 73rd visit in my lifetime. I finally found the courage to go back with a friend of mine. I had no clue what to expect either. We stayed for a few days at Aria and we were actually tourists. We went out to clubs, found ourselves by the pool and walked around the strip. I took a few minutes away from him to go to Bellagio to see if Mikey still worked there and stop at my security box to verify if my envelope was where it should be. When I made my way to the high limit area, I asked the guy working if Mikey was around. He was confused and asked if I had a last name for him and I was shocked that I never found it out. I briefly described what Mikey looked like and he said that he had been working here for seven years and he had never known a Mikey. I remembered the only noticeable thing that Mikey had that was unique, was a small tattoo of a bird on his right hand, a dove. Again, the gentleman shook his head and said he has never known anyone to match that description during his career at Bellagio. I asked another floor man in another pit and he couldn't give me an answer either.

To this day I will never know who Mikey was. Maybe I was delusional back then. Maybe I was that fucked up, intoxicated and caught up in the Vegas lifestyle, that in a way I did drug myself to acquire a friendship with a person that didn't even exist. To have conversations with people that I did think were right there in front of me, but actually never even were. And the more I thought about it, I don't ever remember seeing Mikey touch any of the chips, or talk to the dealers. The few times we were together that I can recall, he was just walking around in a suit and monitoring the area. But then I remembered that morning when I came back to Bellagio to give him the envelope with the bullet inside. He took it from me and I know I shook his hand. Confused, I ran to the cage, gave them my player's card and social security number to get my box out from the vault. After a few minutes had gone by, it arrived. I grabbed the shoebox size piece of steel and opened it up slowly. There was the envelope and I could see the outline of the bullet in the bottom corner of it. I rubbed the surface of it with my finger and a tear fell from my eye. Somehow it made its way to my box one way or the other. I made a promise to myself that day that I would never open this box up ever again. That bullet was worth more to me than any big score in Bobby's Room, or any limo ride or private jet. I told the lady thanks and she made her way back down the hallway and out of my sight.

Maybe it was just a coincidence that day that those two floor men had never heard of Mikey in their career. I am sure Bellagio has thousands of employees and maybe they never overlapped each other. But both of those guys I asked had been there over seven years apiece. Or maybe it's just that Mikey was an angel, a past gambler's soul that wanted to make sure that I was alright when the rest of the world didn't care about me. That he was able to see past my faults and could tell how much I loved everything about the game and the environment I was in all the time, regardless of my constant intoxication. Maybe that tattoo on his hand wasn't a bird, it was his wings. Maybe he was my guardian.

I've had plenty of time to reflect on who I was and the things that I did back then. I can admit that I'll always be an alcoholic of some type. Not the belligerent and chronic asshole that I was, but I do enjoy my glasses of wine every night after a long day at work. Honestly, I don't think I would have been able to live the life I did back then without its presence. Doesn't mean I did anything wrong, doesn't mean I did anything right either. Alcohol just always had to be there wherever I was. Since 2012, I've completed 200 hours of counseling for it, but I know that it'll always be an addiction of mine. I'm just happy that I can control it these days.

I don't gamble anymore either. Which is shocking to everyone including myself. It would probably take a $500k stake these days to get me to leave my job, if that. Personally, I don't ever see that happening. Over the last few years I have been given plenty of offers to play cards again. Some of them have even reached the $100k range. I just don't feel it though. I don't feel that comfort and confidence anymore to go back on the road and play tournaments again.

I'm glad that in 2005 I decided to leave school and go on an adventure that I knew nothing about. I took the biggest risk of my life before I was taking any risks at all if you really think about it. I praise people now that gamble for a living. I don't think that I would ever be able to do it again. Not just because of the things that I went through, but because there's so much more to life.

When it was all said and done and I wrote down a timeline of things, bankroll timeframes that I could recall, sessions that I could put down on paper, loans, expenses and everything else. I came up with $10.5 million. That's the best guess that I can give you as to the amount of money that went in and out of my fingertips in those few years. But the most I ever had at one point was around $1.7 million.

I still get sad sometimes that all of it is gone. It's hard for me now to imagine that I lived such a life. It's difficult to believe what life truly means until you go through such a negative life altering finale. For what it's worth now, I love my life how it has turned out. I don't even want to wonder what I would be doing had I stayed in school and lived a normal life. Everything has just turned out to be ok in the end. Out there in the desert that night after the gun didn't fire, I knew, somehow, that I had to stay alive. I had to keep breathing. Because all of my logic on that drive out there that night, made me think that I would never see a sunrise ever again. I was going to die out there. By myself. I would never be able to go to my favorite restaurant ever again or have conversations with my friends. I would never be able to meet the love of my life and have children with her. I had power over nothing and was helpless. But I got a second chance at life. So that's what I did. I stayed alive and I kept breathing. I have definitely twisted the odds of life where I shouldn't be here right now. But now here I am. In a dark hotel room on a business trip in Kansas City. I have a pizza next to me and an ice cold lemonade on my nightstand. Life is beautiful on how it evolves when you least expect it. I am so sad that I don't have Marie, but I am forever grateful that the future thought of her was with me that night out there in the desert. The thought of the amazing people that had yet to come into my life that would forever change who I was. I've come to terms with what I have to do now. I have to keep waking up every day like I have been these last four years. I have to keep moving and stay positive. Because the sun is going to rise tomorrow, and you just never really know what hand you're going to be dealt.

When I think about the demons, I know that they'll always be with me somehow. Sometimes they were like close friends. If anything, out there in the desert that night when I was laying on top of that car, they helped me make the decision I made. Somehow the most terrifying moment of my life, saved my life. No human should ever want to put a gun to their head to finish themselves. It's the most disappointing thing I ever did in my life. Why the safety was on that day, I'll never know. And no one will ever have an answer to that question either. They live now only within my past. We all have demons inside of us, one way or the other. Some have yet to surface themselves and others will just simply haunt you until your days here have come to an end.

And the devil, he's around somewhere. His temptations, bad decisions, and reoccurring thoughts gave me a career that I don't regret a single day of. And I never will. I would do it all over again with the same results if I was given the chance to. I guess that's just the beauty of it in the end, the artistry. It was an emotional journey that will always be special to me, regardless of how it ended. The only difference between us now, is that he's still drinking some type of poison on the rocks, out there somewhere in the desert. Standing on some distant mountain somewhere overlooking Vegas. I'm sure he's anxiously waiting for me to come back to his side again with a drink in his hand. But he's all by himself from here on out. Because for me, it's safe to say that my glass is finally empty and the ice cubes have melted. But more importantly than anything else, I survived it all. Somewhere between that life changing night out there in the desert and as I write this, through the pain and the birth into my new beginning, finding the ability to fall in love and watching the sun go down beyond the earth any chance I could, he and I took out a few seconds of our new lives to shake hands and finally go our separate ways.

I guess we can call it even.

Made in the USA
Lexington, KY
13 March 2014